Praise for *The Strong Black Woman*

"If ever there was a book for these times, for Black women, for Black People and for all people of all races and genders, *The Strong Black Woman* is it. Both painful and hopeful, instructive over that which could be, and all too often is, destructive, Marita Golden provides, in her words, 'a healing balm' even for those who believe they have no need.

"Through her own often-painful history and revealing glimpses of other women who have had to work through pain many would find unimaginable, Golden's journey is along a road that, in the end, is filled with trees bearing fruit of a very special life and lives, thankfully shared by one of our most powerful writers."

—Charlayne Hunter-Gault, American civil rights activist, journalist, and former foreign correspondent for NPR, CNN, and PBS

"Necessary and relevant, *The Strong Black Woman* shows the time is now to let go of what no longer serves you. Love— whether it is loving others or yourself—is the most important thing. It is a doorway for compassion, kindness, gratitude and well-being. Marita Golden's moving personal narrative invites you to step through a new door; to be with yourself, and ultimately, to love yourself in only the way you know how."

—Bridgitte Jackson-Buckley, blogger, interviewer, memoirist, and author of *The Gift of Crisis*

"In *The Strong Black Woman*, Marita shares her own joys and pains and what has made her the literary force we know. Through the art of storytelling and the wisdom garnered through her research we are able to experience the truth, that the strong Black woman is not just a troupe that is the reflection of our trauma, but is the truth of our brilliance. The book does what Marita has always done, use story to offer Black women a reflection of our lives and a way to grow. *Strong Black Woman* is as much an act of literary activism as every effort that Marita Golden puts forth. Bravo for writing a book that will long benefit us all."

—Zelda Lockhart, author of the novel *Fifth Born*

"*The Strong Black Woman* shatters the myth and the burden that too many of us have carried for too long while holding up villages and fighting for justice. By the end of the first chapter, I was nearly in tears. I was ready to send the book to my mother, sisters, cousins, nieces, and best friends. *The Strong Black Woman* gives us explanations for the pain and histories that our mothers couldn't or wouldn't tell us, a book that is required reading for every person—Black, White, man, woman, and child—who wants to remain healthy and survive in a world that wants otherwise."

—DeNeen L. Brown, award-winning writer for *The Washington Post* and producer of the documentary *Tulsa the Fire and the Forgotten*

The
Strong
Black
Woman

Other Books by Marita Golden

The
Strong
Black
Woman

How a Myth Endangers the Physical and Mental Health of Black Women

By Marita Golden

CORAL GABLES

For permission requests, please contact the publisher at:
Mango Publishing Group
2850 S Douglas Road, 2nd Floor
Coral Gables, FL 33134 USA
info@mango.bz

For special orders, quantity sales, course adoptions and corporate sales, please email the publisher at sales@mango.bz. For trade and wholesale sales, please contact Ingram Publisher Services at customer.service@ingramcontent.com or +1.800.509.4887.

The Strong Black Woman: How A Myth Endangers the Physical and Mental Health of Black Women

Library of Congress Cataloging-in-Publication number: 2021942396
ISBN: (print) 978-1-64250-683-9, (ebook) 978-1-64250-684-6
BISAC category code BIO002010, BIOGRAPHY & AUTOBIOGRAPHY / Cultural, Ethnic & Regional / African American & Black

Printed in the United States of America

This book is dedicated to my grandmother, Molly Reid, my mother, Beatrice Reid, and my sister, Jean Straughn, all Strong Black Women who, in different ways, showed me the way.

To Alicia Garza, Patrisse Cullors, and Opal Tometi, whose love of Black people inspired the Black Lives Matter Movement.

And to Bree Newsome Bass, who on June 27, 2015, scaled a thirty-foot pole to remove the Confederate flag from the South Carolina State House grounds, ten days after the massacre of nine Black people attending a Bible study at Emanuel African Methodist Episcopal prayer meeting by a White supremacist. On July 10, 2015, the Confederate flag was permanently removed.

Table of Contents

Introduction

These essays, meditations, conversations, interviews, and imaginings were written in the spring and summer of 2020, that perilous introduction to pandemic and panic, that distance from and longing for a recent past that suddenly seemed, in memory, like nirvana. This book was born of questions about my health. Its identity is hybrid, fractured, and multi-layered. It is a love letter to Black women, a call to arms, and a balm. Locked down. Locked out. Quarantined. I did what I have always done. I marshalled words to build bridges and break locks separating me from what I needed most, what I have always needed, what we all need—community.

On these pages are musings about Black women's health, but essentially, I am investigating the state of our souls. I cite statistics that claim to measure our physical health and reveal the ways that our ill-health has been designed and defined by others, and ask how we can reclaim it. What does it mean to be a Strong Black Women in this time when we are, as a world, frail, vulnerable, failing? How do we hurt? Where do we hurt? How do we heal? These essays are written in the voice of our sorrow songs and Amen corners in all their uncertainty and cumbersome contradictions.

These essays came to me as though they had been summoned. This is the book I've been waiting to be woman and human enough to imagine and then try to write. To write with humility and bravado, the characteristics that set a writer free to piece together a story. I wanted to write a narrative as sturdy and as useful as a quilt. Speaking of the role of the Black writer, James Baldwin said, "We must tell the truth till we can no longer bear it."

In these pages I have written about the burdens and blessings of Black womanhood until I could no longer bear it. Not because the story is so terrible—rather, because of its river-deep, mountain-high beauty, courage, and grace. I stopped, not because I was finished, but because this, like all stories, is the beginning. It is an invitation for you to cross its portal and tell a story of your own.

We Wear the Mask

The MRI revealed two strokes that I knew nothing about. Two symptomless "silent" strokes that had occurred, according to my doctor, sometime in the past. The MRI revealed the strokes but could not offer clues to when, on two occasions, while I was unaware of it, my brain had been under attack. When the blood supply to my brain was cut off. When, as a result, the essential oxygen and nutrients my brain required to function were denied. When my brain cells were destroyed. When two sections of my brain essentially died.

I sat in the examining room of my doctor, whom my husband and I had been seeing for over twenty years. Dr. Michael Cannaday combines joviality with compassion, and as he sat thumbing through the voluminous records, test results, and paperwork of my file, I saw the concern on his face. We had discussed the implications of the results of the MRI, the possibility of another stroke, or a heart attack, and he told me to add a baby aspirin to prevent blood clots that could cause a stroke to my daily regimen of a multivitamin and the cholesterol and high blood pressure medication I took. I was to immediately make an appointment with my cardiologist to have my heart monitored. And I was to make an appointment to return to his office for an echocardiogram which would scan my heartbeat and identify heart disease. I was given a referral for a carotid duplex scan to identify blockages in my arteries.

I sat in the room, after Dr. Cannaday left to go to his next patient, reeling with emotions. I had done everything right, or thought I had, and it seemed to me that my body was punishing me for it. My husband had suffered two small strokes with heart attacks in the last two years. In both cases, the stroke symptoms (blurred vision, numbness in his arm, slurred speech) struck in a flash, and were gone within sixty seconds the first time and subsided within five minutes the second time. But he knew he'd had a stroke.

In both cases he was hospitalized, given a battery of tests and sent home with modifications to his medications, after three days under the excellent care of a United Nations of doctors and specialists at Washington Hospital Center. My husband was a twenty-four-year survivor of non-Hodgkin's lymphoma, a cancer that originates in the lymphatic system, which supports the disease fighting network in the body. After months of hospitalizations and rigorous chemotherapy and radiation that saved his life, the until-then-dormant diabetes gene that runs in his family activated, and he now lives with Type 2 diabetes.

I was not diabetic, weighed the same as I had in college, exercised regularly, almost religiously, ate healthy, rarely got a cold, had no seasonal allergies. I meditated daily, journaled, and often engaged in days of silence to rejuvenate my spirit. And I had a rich, varied, and deeply satisfying network of friends. Nobody believed I was turning seventy soon. My greatest vulnerability, I thought until that moment in Dr. Cannaday's office, was an A-Type personality. That is what I told myself. But several years earlier, a malignant (cancerous) tumor was found in my rectum during my regular colonoscopy. It was removed, and I did not have to undergo chemotherapy. I followed a regimen, initially of body scans and checkups every six months, that had revealed no further growth and had now evolved into a single annual checkup. I eagerly sailed into those annual visits with my cancer doctor like a hyped-up overachieving student, ready to show off lab tests that would earn me a clean bill of health. So far, they always had. I didn't think of myself as a cancer survivor. A cancerous tumor was found in my rectum, but I wasn't a cancer survivor. Not me.

But I was. I am. Thinking of myself as a *cancer* survivor would have dulled the armor I wore that I worked so hard to keep unscarred and untarnished. And yes, I was on high blood pressure medicine, but I had that under control.

As I sat in Dr. Cannaday's office alone, attempting to absorb the news that I had experienced two strokes, the image of myself that I had crafted over the years as in charge of my body, as nearly invincible, as the poster child for Black female health, vanished. I was dizzy with confusion, and sat attempting to beat back a creeping despair. I had had two strokes.

I was a writer who had spent the last five years researching and writing first a novel, then a major piece of journalism, and finally editing an anthology about the disproportionate impact of Alzheimer's disease on African Americans. I was now too familiar with the "twice as likely syndrome" that resulted in Blacks being twice as likely to develop a majority of the most lethal health conditions, from diabetes to obesity to stroke to heart attack; we lead the way and are often, according to statistics, "twice as likely" to be living with and dying from these disorders. And all of that is one reason we have more Alzheimer's and other dementias. So intellectually I knew my risk. Now I owned it.

Who was I? What else was my body doing? Apparently Black did crack.

I gathered my coat, my purse, and the book I had brought in case of a wait, and walked to the receptionist. The excellent health coverage my husband and I had, thanks to his years teaching in the Washington, DC, public school system, combined with Medicare, meant that I had no co-pay and no reason to do more than simply wave goodbye to Ms. Thomas, the doctor's receptionist and assistant. Instead, as I put on my

coat, I told her in a small, trembling, still-shocked voice what the MRI
had revealed. "They were tiny strokes. So small I had no awareness of
them." I smiled weakly, struggling somehow to make lemonade out of
the lemons I had been handed. Looking over the top of her glasses as
she leaned in close to me, Ms. Thomas shook her head and said, "Small
or big, a stroke is a stroke."

The road to the MRI started a few days after Christmas. Standing up
from my computer, I felt the sudden onslaught of a dizziness that
briefly made it seem that the room was spinning. I felt unstable, and
a bit woozy. But I did not think much about it, since the worst of
the sensations passed quickly. For the next two days, I felt a minor
off-centeredness, reminiscent of sensations I'd had with an ear
infection a year earlier. I called my ear, nose, and throat doctor for
an appointment later in the week. None of my normal activities were
affected, but the dizziness persisted. Then my blood pressure shot
up and I went to an emergency health center in my neighborhood.
During the ten hours I spent in the emergency center, I had an
electrocardiogram that revealed no issues. During the long emergency
room hours of waiting and switching channels on the overhead
television filled with infomercials, my blood pressure went down. Yet,
because of the dizziness, I was sent to a local hospital for tests that the
health center could not provide. By 2:00 a.m., at the hospital, I was
presenting no symptoms and was sent home.

A week later, Dr. Cannaday ordered an MRI in response to the
persistent dizziness. The MRI revealed evidence of two minor strokes
that had occurred sometime in the past. In addition, I underwent a

two-hour hearing test that revealed no problems, and wore a heart
monitor that confirmed that my heart was strong. And none of my
doctors could tell me what the dizziness meant or signaled. Not Dr.
Cannaday. Not the cardiologist. Not my ENT specialist. They all
admitted they simply did not know what had happened to me during
those three days. None of them suspected a stroke. I was concerned,
but relieved to know more about my body and health than I had
known before.

After discussing the dizziness I had experienced and the MRI results
with Dr. Cannaday, I thought my body was punishing me. In reality,
my body was warning me. If not for that bout of dizziness and high
blood pressure, I might not have known that I had had two strokes.
And, although I had not wanted to claim the identity of a cancer
survivor, I already had an appointment for the fall for my annual post-
cancer exam. I was a Strong Black Woman, but clearly not that strong.

My living and aging and thoughts about death are shadowed by
the lives and deaths of my parents, neither of whom lived to be old.
Neither of them lived much longer than the 1970s' established life
expectancy for Black men and women. My mother died at sixty-
three, and my father at sixty-two. They both died when, to my young
adult eyes, they appeared to be healthy. A decade before her death in
1971, my mother had survived and quickly recovered from a cerebral
hemorrhage, a massive stroke that initially left her partially paralyzed
on her right side. In the months before she died, my mother was
overweight and had a "bad knee" that forced her to periodically use
a cane. I knew my mother had health issues, but I never suspected

how precarious her health really was. My mother had been deeply
impacted by the deaths of a succession of friends with whom she had
shared decades-long friendships. Long separated from my father, she
had found a beau in a sixty-nine-year-old divorced neighbor and that
relationship seemed to both thrill and surprise her. She bragged to
anyone who would listen about my achievements as a junior attending
American University. And then, one afternoon, I came home and
found my mother sprawled on the bathroom floor, her brown eyes
open, cloudy, and unseeing. She had been struck, this time fatally, by
another stroke.

My father loved El Producto cigars. The Cuban and Puerto Rican
tobacco leaves of the popular stogy, rolled into an eight-inch-long tube
of what my father considered heaven, perfumed him with a smokey,
sweet aroma that I came to consider my father's signature smell. The
popular brand was the favorite of celebrities from Elvis Presley to
the octogenarian comedian George Burns, who smoked ten a day.
I cherished the colorful paper ring that surrounded the cigar, with
its imprint of a svelte, red-dressed dark-haired woman strumming a
small harp. I'd slip the paper ring on my finger and store my childhood
treasures in the empty cigar box.

Diagnosed with a brain tumor seven years before his death, my father
told his doctor that, as the doctor requested, he'd give up his beloved
El Productos. The tumor gradually shrank, and my father celebrated
what he thought was a reprieve. But he died of a heart attack in his
sleep at 12:15 in the morning of his sixty-second birthday. Abstinence
from the cigar had saved his brain, but the years of inhaling the
comforting yet toxic fumes (and that is what smoking is) had likely
damaged his heart.

My mother died six years short of the sixty-nine-year life expectancy for a Black woman back then. My father lived two years longer than he was predicted to, as a Black man. They had become parents in middle age. Their deaths seemed premature and cruel, and yet…my mother needed to lose forty pounds. She also needed a hobby or interest to engage her mind, to help combat the creeping senility that my uncle suspected she was developing. Years of smoking had ravaged my father's entire body, despite the belief that it only endangers the lungs. I inherited from my parents a genetic predisposition for stroke and heart attack.

My parents' deaths instilled in me an absolute rage to live longer than they did. A rage to live long and well. A rage to do what they never got to do—live to be old. If I had not made a nearly sacred vow to myself in the wake of my parent's deaths that I would live a healthy life, those two silent strokes might have been debilitating rather than silent.

"Black don't crack" is an age-old adage rooted in both science and a chauvinistic in-your-face race pride. Black skin doesn't age like White skin, and in general Black people age, at least on the surface, with a startling grace. The amount of melanin in Black skin is the key. Melanin is a sticky pigment produced by the skin that works like a sunscreen, providing some of the major protection for the skin from UV rays. A specific type of melanin called eumelanin creates a dark skin tone. The more eumelanin your body produces, the darker the skin. Even mixed-race people benefit from the protection eumelanin provides.

I've used the phrase "Black don't crack" when assessing the physical appearance of African American friends who looked a decade (or more) younger than their age. Folks have said it about me. The phrase has a kind of magic power. If you are on the receiving end of the phrase, it feels like an anointing, an affirmation. In a society and world where Black appearance, style, beauty has been mocked, demonized, and questioned, we could always rely on the trump card of skin that the world paradoxically envies for its ability to resist longer than other races the damaging effects of the sun. But the reality is that eventually our skin does age, sag, and wrinkle. And, while not common, Black people can and do develop skin cancer. Our nonchalance about the supposed superpower of our skin often means that we are most often diagnosed in the later stages of the disease.

But we are so much more than our skin. The assertion that Black don't crack becomes for Black women the belief that not just our skin, but our minds and bodies, don't crack. They don't crack and shouldn't and won't. But Black women are not just cracking. We are broken. The three leading causes of death for African American women are heart attack, cancer, and stroke. Black women are three times as likely to die of a heart attack as White women. Too many of us, of all ages and classes, are overweight, obese, have high blood pressure, are stressed out, diabetic, don't get annual checkups, and lack ways to positively "crack" and then rebuild ourselves.

Our bodies, souls, and spirits are a map, a testimony to the ravages of our enslavement, the cruel legacy of legal segregation and lack of access to wealth, good employment, stable housing, and good health care. And our psyches have been twisted and turned inside out by the stories we tell ourselves. And the stories that are told about us. Stories that have sometimes saved and sometimes sabotaged us. The Strong Black Woman. The Angry Black Woman. The Black woman

who says yes to everyone but herself. The Black woman who believes
Jesus and only Jesus is the answer to every problem, who rejects the
idea that therapists, doctors, self-care are also part of Jesus's plan. The
Superwoman. The Invincible Superwoman. We've had to be strong.
We have good reason to be angry. We say yes over and over to our
families because the world so often tells them no. And who wouldn't
want to be a Superwoman?

I was twenty-one years old and my mother was dying. She lay
comatose in a bed in a rehabilitation center for six months, wasting
away before my eyes. I was a raise-the-Black-power-fist, Afro-wearing,
militant activist, and a B-plus-average student attending American
University, and I had already started wearing the mask. The Strong
Black Woman mask. During the agonizing months of my mother's
illness, death, and the grieving that followed, I told only one person
what I was going through—my best friend. Louise and I had attended
DC's Western High School together, where we worked on the student
newspaper and shared our plans for life after high school, life after
college, life as grown women. At American University, we studied
philosophy, English, and science, and discovered love and sex and
heartbreak with boyfriends returning to the US after a stint in the
Peace Corps, or who were from an African nation we had read about
in books and hoped to visit one day. We became young women. We
became young Black women. Together. Louise was the only person
with whom I didn't wear *the mask*.

What I remember:

Attending classes and continuing to excel, in fact, tackling my classes with even more rigor and vigor as my mother lay dying. Classes where I was always prepared, and always had an opinion (usually informed), were my lifeline in this season of dying. I wrote papers, attended meetings of the Organization of African American Students at the American University (OASATAU) and the Black Student Union, wrote a column for the *Eagle*, the student newspaper, and worked twenty hours a week in the Financial Aid office. And on campus, nobody besides Louise knew that my mother was dying.

I was twenty-one and already I was a Strong Black Woman. Being a Strong Black Woman meant that you "handled your business." You did what you had to do, no matter what. My mother was dying, but I had to continue to be a successful student. Being a Strong Black Woman meant that you didn't bother others unnecessarily with your pain. In the small apartment where I lived with my mother, my nights were sleepless, tear-filled meltdowns in which in the dark I whispered, shouted, and screamed the questions I was terrified to ask in the light of day.

Why would I soon be a motherless child? How would I go on?

I woke from those nights wrapped in sheets that held me captive, broke free, showered, put on the mask, and prepared for the performance that would take me through the day. There was a counseling service on campus, but I never once thought of using it. I was estranged from my father. My sister was ten years older than me, a divorced single mother of five sons, and we were distanced in our grief by old jealousies and suspicions. My uncle was a minister, but I didn't ask him for comfort. My uncle, the emotional and material anchor of my mother's siblings, could be judge, jury, and executioner with one glance. But if I woke every day to the knowledge that my mother was dying, he woke each day aware that he was losing the older sister who had taken him into her home, helped him "get on his feet" in Washington when he followed her migration from Greensboro, North Carolina. There was a vulnerability that my uncle only revealed when he popped open a can of Schlitz beer at our kitchen table. And now he was grieving too. And he was wearing his own mask.

I'd rarely, if ever, seen my mother cry. Maybe she, too, cried in the dark. How I wish she had cried in the light. Despite all that she had made of her life after her arrival in Washington, DC, as part of the great migration of African Americans from the South, there was a lot she could have cried about.

My mother was, like many Black women of her era, a domestic worker. She cleaned the homes and apartments of families of DC's White upper class. But her knack for hitting it big, winning at "the numbers," the unofficial lottery of her day, provided her with the money to rent and own several boarding houses in DC's Columbia Heights neighborhood. With my taxi-driver father, she provided my sister and me a childhood of grand three-story Victorian houses. We were well-fed, clothed, doted on, and denied little.

My mother left her first husband in Greensboro, a fact about her life I did not learn until years after her death, when one of her oldest friends told me. Her second husband suffered from alcoholism. After they parted, he was committed to St. Elizabeths mental hospital in Southeast Washington, and she visited him regularly. My father, her third husband, was a womanizer. He was like a drug habit my mother couldn't shake, and to whom she lost nearly everything. But I never saw her cry. Out of my view, after they separated, my parents hammered out a truce. I never knew what all this cost my mother. The price she paid. My mother kept on stepping, outran despair, and handled her business. And I was her youngest daughter. The daughter who did the same.

My mother's death was followed a year and a half later by the death of my father, five months before my graduation from the Graduate School of Journalism at Columbia University. At the age of twelve, my mother, beaming proudly at my love of reading and writing, had told me that one day I was going to write a book. My father raised me to be as bold and adventurous as a boy was expected to be. They both had always talked to me, no matter my age, as though I was intelligent and deserved to hear the truth as they saw it. They encouraged my curiosity. I had watched their lives go up in flames more than once and witnessed their talent for walking through the fire and coming out scorched but still able to envision a way to start over. And so, because I was their child, I put their deaths behind me (I thought) and began striding through doors once bolted against African Americans, to accomplish all they had told me I could.

But when I fell for Femi, a Nigerian graduate student in architecture, I knew I hadn't put their deaths behind me at all. He was as ebony-beautiful as was my father. And he possessed the same daunting mystique of emotional distance that my mother and my father's "other" women had clearly found irresistible in my father. His culture revolved around family in ways that made our union inevitable.

I'd begun publishing articles in *Essence* magazine and was soon to be hired as an associate producer for New York's PBS station, but none of that had eradicated the identity I held like a secret swaddled in my heart. I was an orphan, and I feared I would always feel like one.

After four years living with Femi in Nigeria, I would look back on
our marriage from the vantage point of its demise and realize that in
it I had created a hiding place, a womb. The marriage ended when
I was ready to be reborn. I wrote the first words of my first book as
a hardened veteran of loss. I had lost my parents, and a child in a
miscarriage in Nigeria, before giving birth successfully to my son, and
then I lost my marriage.

All of the varying definitions of the word *lost* defined my feelings
during that time: *1. Unable to find one's way, not knowing one's
whereabouts; unable to be found; very confused or in great difficulties; 2.
Denoting something that has been taken away or cannot be recovered.*
And I had yet to talk with a therapist about any of this. I had been
stripped bare of a sense of emotional wholeness, but resilience was my
default setting.

While working in the pressure-cooker environment at the PBS station,
I had begun the practice of Transcendental Meditation. Twice a day,
for twenty minutes, I meditated, using a mantra to calm and still my
mind and thoughts. The twenty-minute sessions provided rest as deep
as REM sleep and left me refreshed and focused. I have meditated
nearly all my adult life, and this was the first step I took to ensure some
sense of mental health. Meditation slowed me down, improved my
sleep, gave me more energy, and in real and tangible ways improved
the quality of my life. Over the years I would go on silent retreats,
practice days of silence on my own, study Buddhism, and practice
different forms of Buddhist meditation as well as mindfulness. As
a twenty-eight-year-old woman who felt like a wounded warrior,
Transcendental Meditation helped me enormously, but it did not help
me integrate into my life in a healthy way the grief that haunted me.

When I did see a therapist, I was driven to her office because I couldn't write the memoir for which I had a contract and a deadline. I was uncustomarily blocked, and I knew why. The book required that I examine and recount my doomed marriage. Several visits in, I finally named the reason for the wall inside me: anger at myself and my husband for the ways in which we had failed each other. The sessions were cathartic and blasted through the wall of pain that I'd built and that encased my heart. I left the therapist's office ready to write. I had work to do, a career to build, and so I decided there was no time to share the grief I carried for my parents and that stillborn child. Once again, I'd put what I could not bear to face behind me, but it haunted every step I took.

———

As much as my writing ambitions drove me, the love of my son and being his single parent was the primary organizing principle of those years. After our divorce, his father still lived in Nigeria, and I felt emotionally and physically estranged from him. The trauma and drama of our separation and divorce made me hesitant to reach out to his extended family in New York. So I tackled being a single mother the way I tackled anything and everything that was important to me—head on. I was raising Michael against the 1990s backdrop of the drug wars and violence racking inner-city communities, and the knowledge that, in the city that was our home, Washington, DC, each year, 400 people, mostly young Black males, were murder victims. *Four hundred. Each year.*

In one of my mother's oldest friends, "Aunt Bert," Michael had a caring surrogate grandmother. When he was twelve, I got him a "Big

Brother," an African American investment banker with a desire to
"give back." Seeking to widen our network of emotional support,
I started a single parents' group with eight Black women and one
man. We'd meet monthly to share our concerns about our lives
and children, take them on field trips, or just let them do their own
thing in that month's host's backyard or basement while we kicked
back upstairs.

I was talented at creating surrogate family networks to support me as
a single mother and in the world of work. While teaching at a well-
known Virginia university, I formed a support group with three female
Black faculty from that school, one from a university in Maryland,
and one from DC. We were literary scholars, poets, novelists, brilliant
Black women publishing in our field, doing groundbreaking work as
we contributed to the contemporary canon of Black women's writing
and enhanced the understanding of it. Teaching was my passion, and I
was buoyed by working with White students who enrolled in my Black
literature classes, some of whom shared with me their desire to reject
family legacies of racist thought and action, and Black students who
were empowered by reading the memoirs of Malcolm X and Audre
Lorde. I tried my best to support all my students, whether they were
dealing with daily microaggressions and a sense of isolation on the
campus, or in need of validation of their writer's voice.

Those five women and I were valuable assets on our campuses. We had
changed and enlarged not just how the academy looked, but what it
meant and the ideas that could be pursued on its grounds. Still, some
of our White colleagues deemed us affirmative-action hires whose
qualifications were suspect. There were few African Americans in
positions of authority at our universities. I learned that the hallowed
halls of a college campus can be as cutthroat as a corporate boardroom.

Our frequent potluck dinners confirmed our intelligence, our beauty, and our creativity as we discussed our in-progress work, vented, let off steam, and gave ourselves over to the healing balm of friendship. With community activist and bibliophile Clyde McElvene, I cofounded first the African American Writers Guild and later the Zora Neale Hurston/Richard Wright Foundation to give Black writers what I craved—spaces in my life where I was seen, where I was nurtured, where I could evolve. The Hurston/Wright Foundation would grow into an institution offering workshops, public readings, and awards for published and unpublished Black writers, from college writers to veteran authors. As I write this, the foundation is celebrating thirty years of creating community for Black writers.

From a distance, it looked like I had it *going on*. While these efforts provided real satisfaction and some healing, my love life, my relationships with men, were scenes of serial carnage. Over and over I was drawn to, and invited into my life, the same emotionally distant, withholding men. Men who were drawn to me because of my accomplishments while simultaneously hating me for them. Men who were in need of repair and who fulfilled my need to fix things and people. It was my son who set in motion a process that would force me to look inside for a change. He wanted to be in relationship with his father and his father's family. Wanted to know more about my family. I was a genius at creating surrogate families while shrugging off the harder job of being a member of my actual family. I engaged a prominent Howard University therapist to work with my son around the pain he was suffering about the absence of his father, despite the Big Brother and the single parents' group. The pain he was suffering about me. He had seen both the acclaim I garnered as a writer and the wreckage of my relationships with men. He wondered what was wrong. He knew I wasn't happy, and that knowledge filled him with confusion and guilt.

Soon the therapist was working with me as well, and it was in her
office, twenty years after the deaths of my parents, that I finally
cracked—cracked open, cracked wide open. I had blasted through
the wall of anger I harbored against my husband with the first
therapist years earlier, but another wall remained—the wall of anger
at my parents for not just dying, but, in my eyes, abandoning me.
On that wall was scrawled this fervent belief: If they had loved me,
truly loved me, they would never have died when I was on the cusp
of womanhood. Their deaths confirmed the secret fear that I was
undeserving of their love. If I hadn't deserved their love and loyalty
then, I didn't deserve a man who could be loving and loyal now. I
couldn't find love in a man because I had yet to accept my ability to
love and cherish myself. First. I was a phantom, a skeletal half-woman
seeking a man to complete me. And since I was half a woman, I fell
over and over again for a half-formed man.

I had been running a marathon. The destination away from the past,
preferably at warp speed. Don't look back, because there was nothing
there I could use. Don't look back, because I would only see betrayal
and loss. Don't look back, because I had to keep my eye on the prize I
was running toward. But I was running in place. Refusing to touch the
skin of feelings still raw and wounded. Running in place hypnotized by
the illusion that movement in and of itself was progress.

Those sessions with that therapist literally launched me into a *whole*
life. One in which I seemingly met myself for the first time, a life
in which I repaired relationships with my family. Michael and I
would journey to Nigeria to see his father and establish a deep and
meaningful relationship with his Nigerian family living in the US. I
still yearned for a soulmate, but I now knew that in the end I was my
ultimate partner. And then I met Joe, my second husband. A whole
man, looking for a whole woman.

While writing this, I asked my forty-two-year-old son if he
remembered ever seeing me cry. I anxiously awaited his response by
email. His one-sentence response assured me that he had. In a follow-
up call, we talked about that time. Seeing me cry as a result of a terrible
choice he had made, my son told me, he saw me as helpless. The
mother who had been a bulwark in his life could not save him from the
consequences of his personal decisions. He saw my tears and learned
that he was responsible for the mistakes he made, and that a mother's
love couldn't and shouldn't save him from bearing his own private
cross. He knew he wouldn't bear it alone. But he had to bear it.

Like many Black women, I will tell you that I never saw my mother
cry. Memory is so fickle, so malleable, and has been proven to be in
scientific studies of it so unreliable, that we now know that pretty
much everything we think we remember may be partially or totally
false. Of course, I saw my mother cry. When she saw my father angrily
walk out the door after an argument. At her mother's funeral.

However, *cry* becomes a synonym for being unafraid to admit to
confusion, weakness, to plead for help, for the ability of mothers to
say to their children, "I don't know what to do." Many of us have
seen our mothers pray. On their knees. And they have taught us to
do the same. But when they pray, they are supplicants expecting an
answer, a remedy from a mystical, mysterious force that has gained
their allegiance because it is so deeply unknown and unknowable.
When they place their hands on our trembling shoulders, look into our
frightened eyes, and say the words "I don't know what to do," there is
no expectation of immediate relief, only a willingness to submit to the
darkness of the unknown and a determination to stumble through it.

Those words inform us that we can survive not knowing what to do.
Survival can test and challenge and disappoint us; it can as well leave a
bitter taste. Survival may give us wings and show us the way. And most
of us will survive saying and hearing the words that are admission and
invitation, "I don't know what to do"—words that can imbue us with
a sense of charity and understanding toward our mothers and save us
from feeling fear as we see the first shadows of our own dark days and
nights. Because we so rarely witness this, we say we have never seen
our mothers cry.

The mask is diabolical and dynamic. It becomes reflexive and
theatrical. Even as we convince ourselves that it fits us perfectly, it
feels more like the grip of a snare. A kind of emotional neuroplasticity
that allows us to absorb higher and higher levels of pain. Endurance is
proof of our strength. We don't have to remove the mask, just adjust
it around the edges or find a larger size. Until the mask disintegrates,
turns to ash, as all lies must in the end. The mask, unremoved, can
irreparably harm the relationships we most care about.

I felt nearly invincible wearing my mask. As a writer, my job and my
calling were to control the narrative. And that's what the mask allowed
me to do—control the narrative I presented to the world. I was a
Black woman and I had no other choice. Sometimes I felt like I had
been born wearing the mask of the Strong Black Woman. It was part
of the required uniform as I taught at a historically White university,
as I raised my son against a cacophony of voices that relentlessly
questioned my competence as a single mother, and as I held at arm's
length any man willing to enfold me in his arms while I wept for
reasons known and unknown.

When writing, there is the narrative you know and the one you
to surrender to. The narrative that you plot, and outline, and the

narrative that has a thunderous voice you either cannot or refuse to hear. The narrative that you grow into and that you often resist is inevitably the soul of the narrative, the essence of story itself. The stifled questions, the unaddressed doubts, are the first cracks in the seams of the mask that will uncover your shattered self.

I had spent most of my adult life becoming the almost-seventy-year-old woman sitting in my doctor's office trying to find her center after learning she had had two strokes, who had become, through every twist and turn of her life, a New Age Strong Black Woman. A woman who could handle her business and ask for help, who could create her own support systems, and who saw caring for her mental health as part of her daily regimen. It wasn't easy. It isn't easy. I wanted to know why.

Six Ways of Looking at a Myth

"A Strong Black Woman doesn't let a tear stain her face."
—Unknown

"But what of Black women? I most sincerely doubt if any other race of women could have brought its finest up through so devilish a fire."
—W.E.B. DuBois

"I'm convinced that Black women possess a special indestructible strength that allows us to not only get down, but to get up, to get through, and to get over."
—Janet Jackson

"Usually when people talk about the strength of Black women, they ignore the reality that to be strong in the face of oppression is not the same as overcoming oppression, that endurance is not to be confused with transformation."
—bell hooks

"You may shoot me with your words
You may cut me with your eyes
You may kill me with your hatefulness
But still, like air, I rise."
—Maya Angelou, from "Still I Rise"

"Black women could hardly strive for weakness. They had to
become strong, for their families and their communities needed
their strength to survive. Harriet Tubman, Sojourner Truth, Ida
B. Wells, and Rosa Parks are not exceptional Black women as
much as they are epitomes of Black womanhood."
—Angela Davis

The Glass Half Empty

Scientific studies show a direct link between racial discrimination and
chronic disease. The stress induced by coping with racism becomes
biologically embedded and literally flows through the body like blood.

The mortality rate for babies born to Black mothers with a master's or
doctoral degree is far worse than the mortality rate for babies born to
White mothers with less than an eighth-grade education.

Black women are slightly less likely to have breast cancer, yet are 40
percent more likely to die from it.

Four out of five Black women are overweight or obese.

One in four middle-aged Black women has diabetes.

African Americans are twice as likely to die from heart disease and stroke as Whites.

The fastest-growing segment of the population developing Alzheimer's and other dementias is Black women.

The Glass Half Full

After passage of the Affordable Care Act, access to health care among Black Americans increased dramatically. Doctors say that access to health care is the number one determinant of health.

Black women lead all women in participation in the labor force.

Black women have the largest voter turnout rates.

Black women represent the fastest growing segment of women-owned businesses.

Black women in the corporate world report higher rates of interest in holding leadership positions than White women.

Civil suits by Black female workers formed the basis for federal sexual harassment law.

The activism of a Black woman, Tarana Burke, inspired the #MeToo Movement.

The Strong Black Woman Syndrome, which requires that Black women perpetually present an image of control and strength, is a response to combination of daily pressures and systemic racist assaults. As we live and deal with racism and sexism, the Strong Black Woman response becomes an automatic response. We see this as strength. The world does too. Buttressed and buffeted, sometimes from all sides, we go on, move on, tamping down suffering and complaint. But the price must be paid. The Strong Black Woman syndrome silences the healthy and necessary expression of pain and vulnerability. We are neither indestructible nor invincible. There is no one-size-fits-all Strong Black Woman suit that we can slip into in the shadows, ready to vanquish threats.

The Strong Black Woman was forged in the stinking, squalid hole of a slave ship, on the auction block, in an enslaved woman's ragged rush and run to freedom, nursing White babies instead of our own, when we were defined not really as "women," not like White women were, when it was asserted by Whites that because we were enslaved women we couldn't be "raped," when we were forced to work from dawn to dusk, and to carry and bear any weight, fainting in the grip of "the spirit" in a pew on Sunday morning, becoming against the odds "the first Negro woman to___," doing the grunt work of organizing behind the scenes for civil and human rights, training a White man who would take our job and then become our boss, standing shocked and silent at the news of the deaths of Trayvon Martin, Eric Garner, Sandra Bland, telling our daughters for the millionth time they have to be twice as good, basking in the acceptance and understanding of sister circles, where we are renewed, but where the cycle of adherence to the identity of the Strong Black Woman is also often reinforced.

The history of African American men is a history of systemic attacks on and success at crippling their power and potential. Denied equal opportunity for generations, glass-ceilinged beneath the lowest-status jobs, harshly policed and imprisoned, Black men have been unable in many pockets of the African American community to uplift themselves and provide for and enrich their families. The history of African American women is the same history of being victimized by attempts to cripple our power and potential. We have had to step into the breach to support ourselves and our children, often without the consistent partnership of Black men.

The Strong Black Woman is myth and fact. It is internalized so deeply that even little Black girls are treated like, and assumed to be, miniature Strong Black Women. It is myth because its endurance rests on our need to assert control in the midst of the chaotic storm of racism, individual and systemic. It is myth because it rests on the foundation of tears we don't shed, pain we deny. It is myth because it is so deeply embedded in the collective unconscious of Black women that it is assumed and goes largely unchallenged.

All of life begins with, is defined by, and even ends with, a story. The stories and myths we create and repeat become sacred. They are designed to make and keep us strong. But stories are elastic, and require revision over time or they risk becoming brittle, dissolving into crumbs that leave us famished rather than fed. Stories are so powerful because at their core they are aspirational, codifying what we long to be if we lived in a world where anything really was possible. *Black women have made ourselves the heroes we dream of.*

The Strong Black Woman is fact. The resilience, both emotional and physical, of Black women has populated our history with a cavalcade of models of intelligence, genius, and creativity. We can look at the women in our families, in our neighborhoods, and see unsung heroes, unheralded masters of making everyday miracles, and witness who and what we are at our best. Black women have been "faking it till they made it" for generations, long before social scientists began studying how confidence can be physically expressed and internalized as a natural response.

There is myth. There is fact. There is reality. And there is the collision between all three. Despite our belief in our emotional resilience, which is real but exaggerated, our health metrics are dismal. We are impacted disproportionately by poor housing, lack of high-paying employment options, poor education, food apartheid, polluted environments, and an absence of medical facilities in our communities or insufficient medical coverage. Decades of both an *overinvestment* by federal and state and local governments, in policies that enforced and encouraged racial and economic segregation, and an *absence of investment* in Black people, has created environments where too many Black people do not thrive. And finally, medical and psychological studies have shown that permanent race-related stress is a more powerful factor than other occasional life stressors (divorce, job loss, death of a loved one) in creating poor health. The stress of coping with racism becomes a toxin that infiltrates the body, creating an incubator for other diseases.

Dr. Georgia Willie-Carnegie, a partner in Capital Cardiology Consultants, one of the country's oldest Black cardiology practices, told me the cruel math of living in America as a Black person of any economic class means that, while heart disease is the number one killer of all Americans, African Americans are especially vulnerable. "Hypertension and high blood pressure lead to stroke, kidney failure (renal disease), and heart disease," she told me." I have to remind women to listen to their bodies. We're so busy helping others we show up in the emergency room or the doctor's office at the last minute, often when treatment is least effective."

The Strong Black Woman, as an article of faith and presentation, complicates our quest for good health. Our humanity, our individuality, is erased. Uncertainty, self-doubt, confusion become taboo. And the very belief we are certain will save us is killing us.

Both Sides Now

Black women often fail to seek mental health care. This is fact, not conjecture. Only one-third of Black Americans who need mental health care receive it. The former First Lady—or, as she is known in the Black community, "First Lady Forever"—Michelle Obama, has spoken openly and passionately about the stigma attached to mental health crises and the need to address and respond to our mental health needs. In the African American community, that stigma is generations old.

We've all heard family members described as "a little touched in the head," "crazy," "dangerous." The stigma is so potent among some that it has been believed that mental illness was contagious. Black women who refused to follow traditional norms of female behavior have been routinely written off as "crazy bitches."

The culturally accepted and promoted belief that Black women don't need help makes asking for help an act that can marginalize us in our families, and even in our friendship circles. We are true believers that our resilience, and toughness, our survival skills, equip us with all we need to get through a crisis. *Alone. "The strength that enabled us to survive enslavement, passed down through our ancestors for generations, will see us through."*

Combine that with the still-prevalent belief, among many African Americans of all economic classes, in the definitive power of prayer alone to make everything alright. Some Christians are suspicious of psychotherapy and view it as dangerously secular. Their faith teaches that enough faith in God, unshakable belief in Jesus as your savior, and dedicated prayer is mightier than any depression, anxiety, or breakdown. *"Only a God of boundless power could reward our faith in Him by allowing us to endure in the face of our history. That God and that God alone can provide all the help we need."* These italicized statements are paraphrases of dogma I have heard repeated by Black folk all my life. And then there is the famous gospel song "Come on in the Room," whose lyrics assert, "Jesus is my doctor and he writes out all my prescriptions, he gives me all my medicine in the room. Tell my doctor I said come on in the room…"

Discussing this project with a fellow writer, she laughed with a combination of bitterness and awe as she said, "Most Black women in America are rooted in Christian dogma whose not-so-subtle message is that Black women have been anointed by God to bear a heavy load. I wish Black women would realize being a Strong Black Woman is not a mandate from on high. If anything, it comes from the devil."

Just for flavor, let's add to this toxic brew the well-deserved suspicion of a medical industry, founded centuries ago on experimentation on enslaved Black people, that for decades sterilized Black women without their knowledge, from 1932–1972 denied treatment of syphilis to Black men being studied in the infamous Tuskegee Syphilis Study, and today remains mired in implicit and explicit bias that impacts everything from visits in the doctor's office to clinical trials. The insidious belief that Black women feel less pain than White women is still prevalent in the medical profession.

Dr. Thomas A. LaVeist, Dean of the School of Public Health and Tropical Medicine at the University of New Orleans, has said, "Distrust of the medical industry is built into the social DNA of Black culture." But Pastor Mike Carrion of the Promised Land Covenant Church in the South Bronx, speaking of the mental health needs of his African American parishioners as they faced mounting deaths and loss

of loved ones to the coronavirus, said, "We need the person of God and
we need a God-given therapist to navigate our brokenness."

As I sought to find answers to my mini-health crisis of dizziness and
high blood pressure, I sailed from one medical specialist to another,
unworried about co-pays or appointments. I had access. Lack of access
is the match tossed onto the bonfire of obstacles to meaningful mental
health care for Black women which sets the pile on fire.

The response to the Affordable Care Act, a program that was overdue,
and flawed, nonetheless, proved that if people are encouraged to take
care of their health and obstacles are removed, they will work to get
well and stay healthy. I know women whose lives were saved because
they were covered by Obamacare. You shouldn't have to have a "good
job," live in a community like mine, where I am surrounded by clinics
and medical institutions, or have a certain zip code to have easy access
to mental health options. But this is America, and you do.

But let's stop for a moment. A moment in which we take a breath.
This odyssey began in my doctor's office. In learning truths about
my health and my body. I yearned for answers, but I also longed for
community. I am an echo of a much larger story about Black women's
health. A story that cannot be told using only statistics. Statistics are
the proverbial hammer looking for a nail. Blunt, cowing doubters into
silence, statistics are the road always taken. But anecdote, confession,
testimony, witness, memory (false or true), hindsight, revision, all
expand the tale statistics offer. African Americans have been defined as
a problem so often that we automatically lapse into that self-definition.
We wear it like skin. We are not the problem. We *face* an enduring
problem. And so the story of Black women's health needs to be told
by Black women and told in the language of our choosing, and if that
language is confounding and contradictory and precise and as loose

and gymnastic as a poem, so be it. The story is caught in our throats. It
has been locked away for safekeeping. It has a gun pressing against its
temple. Every day, somewhere, it breaks free. We can force statistics
to do *our* bidding, to travel the road not taken. I wanted to know what
Black women say about their mental health. I wanted our voices to be
the final answer.

Dr. Joy Harden Bradford, an Atlanta-based clinical psychologist, has
her hands literally on the pulse of Black women's mental health. Her
mental health platform, Therapy for Black Girls, connects her thirty-
two thousand followers on social media and her website—whose ages
range from eighteen to fifty-five—with nearly eight hundred African
American therapists and psychologists around the country. Her
weekly podcasts tackle topics as diverse as talking to children about
race and handling anxiety and depression. And her weekly Sunday
Sweet Tea email letters offer commentary on all variety of media
showcasing the lives and achievements of Black women, and links to
articles and information about African American health and wellness,
all in the alluring voice of a compassionate clinical psychologist who is
also your best friend.

When I asked Dr. Harden Bradford about the American Psychological
Association study that found that only one-third of Black Americans
who need mental health care receive it, she told me, "The stigma
against seeking therapy is still active in the Black community. Some
parents still say 'pray it away,' and many who seek therapy are not
supported by their families. The Strong Black Woman syndrome
has been a gift, it's given us resilience and acts as a protector against

pain, but we get trapped in a kind of armor and it's hard to experience real feelings. We don't pay attention to what is really happening to us. I want to make mental health accessible and help Black women realize that we have to foster mental health and not wait for a mental illness crisis."

Still, too often, Dr. Harden Bradford acknowledges that, when Black woman finally decide to seek professional mental health treatment, they are greeted by a system that is as likely to reject their health care plan as to accept it. This is what happens in a society that has made health care a privilege, not a right.

Lauren Carson turned her mental health crisis into a mission to promote mental health literacy among Black girls aged thirteen to nineteen. Lauren attempted suicide. Twice. Now she is Executive Director of Black Girls Smile, a nonprofit that works with schools, social service agencies, and other nonprofits offering workshops in public schools and after-school programs in cities around the country, including Washington, DC, New York, and Atlanta.

The child of a prosperous middle-class Black family, her father is a physician, and her mother works in public health. Lauren was a smart overachiever who remembers, nonetheless, "showing signs of clinical depression at twelve, but not being diagnosed until I was fifteen."

Lauren experienced the sadness, hopelessness, and withdrawal typical of clinical depression, a biological, psychological disorder that changes brain function. After the formal diagnosis, there was

medication and talk therapy, but upon entering the University of
Virginia, where she would major in psychology, she stopped going to
therapy and taking medication. The added pressures of a heavy course
load and watching her father go overseas for the first time, as an army
doctor, sent her spiraling into a depression that led to her first suicide
attempt, followed by another attempt a year later. Both times she was
hospitalized. She said, "I didn't learn about my family's history of
clinical depression until pretty late in all this."

The activist in Lauren was born when she began talking openly with
friends and family, telling those willing to listen that she struggled
and lived with depression. After graduating from the University
of Virginia, she went to New York to work in finance and began
immersing herself in learning all she could about mental health,
especially mental health and Black girls. When President Barack
Obama launched My Brother's Keeper, an initiative to support and
mentor boys of color, Lauren felt there needed to be an emphasis on
the lives of Black girls.

Helping young Black girls build self-esteem and develop the skills
to achieve and maintain mental health is the primary thrust of the
programs that Black Girls Smile offers, in classes from meditation,
stress management, decision-making, and parental relations to
nutrition. Looking back, Lauren says, "Before I came out about my
clinical depression, I felt isolated, I felt ashamed. And since I didn't
tell anybody, I couldn't get help when I needed it. The Strong Black
Woman syndrome drains you. Your tank may not be empty, but it's
never full. When we speak at schools, we see young girls in elementary,
middle school, and high school already modeling the syndrome."

Complicating the work of Black Girls Smile is that Black children
are routinely considered and treated as though they are much older.

Stories of Black toddlers suspended from preschool, Black third graders handcuffed and arrested for minor infractions of school rules, twelve-year-old Tamir Rice shot while holding a toy gun, all send the message to Black children that they are a threat. In addition, it is not uncommon for Black children to act as caregivers for younger siblings to help out a single parent or overworked parents. The job of parenting younger siblings, and the praise they receive for doing so, combined with the messages young Black children receive about their worth and value from the larger society, embeds the Strong Black Woman mentality in Black girls.

As Black women navigate the mental health care system, Lauren said, "We might not get diagnosed, we might not get treated, and we might not get the right treatment. Through many years of treatment and therapy, I learned that I had never been taught how to cope with my difficulty, so I had no skills to handle it."

Lauren has realized that healing is a prescription that has to be filled every day. "I still have bad days and I monitor myself, with medication and therapy when I need it. But there have been blessings and grace in my journey." By making herself and her talents a gift to others, Lauren gains strength as she lives with a diagnosis for which there is no cure, despite effective treatments. From the raw material of clinical depression, Lauren Carson molded a life of purpose and passion. She evolved from victim to advocate, and is bringing other "Black girls" with her and equipping them to do the same.

Sasha Jackson nearly drowned at the beach when she was eight. She was a victim of sexual molestation at ten. Today she swims competitively in the same cold, unpredictable waters of the Atlantic Ocean that almost took her life. And she has been a therapist healing others, and herself, for twenty years. In her practice, where she sees many African American, Caribbean, and African women, Sasha says part of her work involves allying the fears of clients that, since they have come to see her, that means they are "crazy."

She works with clients to dismantle a host of feelings that create a barrier to the often slow and incremental process of therapy. For these women, seeing a therapist is a major decision, often months or even years in the making. For some, it may be the first time they have ever taken such a definitive and demanding step toward caring for themselves.

Among the most common reservations her Black female clients share are: not valuing therapy and feeling guilt over using family resources for it; fearing that they are exaggerating their problems; the shame of being judged; feeling that they should be able to solve their problems on their own; guilt about exposing family secrets; feeling that they should just ignore the problem as they have done in the past; the fear of losing control. These are anxieties that many women who are hesitant to seek out a therapist feel, no matter their race, but they are heightened for Black women. And an additional concern for Black women, born of history and experience, is that they will be judged "more ill" than White women and treated with more severe drugs for a longer time.

Sasha is a survivor of sexual assault who lives with and manages continuing depression and anxiety, and as a practitioner who works with assault victims, I wondered how she finds and maintains inner peace and contentment.

"Years of therapy have helped me a lot," she said. Recently she sought out a therapist for her own treatment when working with a client who triggered memories of her own trauma. "Therapy has helped me process my trauma, helped me talk about it in a nonjudgmental way and to see the wider dimensions of it. It has definitely helped me heal. I can see my family, I can see my trauma, in a much broader context. My therapist is a feminist, womanist, Liberation Theology advocate, so we talk about the whole spectrum of things that have impacted me, my family, and my experience. I guess I would say that for me, inner peace is being in contact with my actual authentic emotions, knowing what truly works for me and acting on that. Feeling that what I give is enough. So many Black women don't know that what they give, especially to their families, is priceless, so they just keep giving and giving."

The body that was nearly swept away, that bore sexual assault, is now a body that Sasha has made strong through swimming competitions and cycling races, and an active practice of supporting her mental health. "I read somewhere," she said, "that the body doesn't lie, that it has its own intelligence." Sasha has listened to her body, its secrets and its truth.

As I searched for the voices of Black women actively addressing the negative health impact of the Strong Black Woman syndrome, I was heartened to find a growing body of work addressing the issue, from memoirs to scholarly studies and texts. One of the most revealing and troubling studies was conducted by Dr. Kanika Bell, a psychologist and Associate Professor in the Department of Psychology at Clark Atlanta University.

When we spoke, she had just returned from a three-day retreat in
the mountains, living in her own life the advice she gives her clients.
"I'm part of a collective of Black women psychologists in Atlanta and
we regularly get together as a group [that is] a kind of sister circle,"
Dr. Bell explained. "We get together as Black women who treat Black
women, and we do the things we tell our clients to do in terms of self-
care. But we also find ourselves struggling with many of the issues that
our clients present. We are where they are. We have been where they
have been. Our clients talk about the same things we talk about."

Dr. Bell surveyed fifty women who identified as Black or African
American who were either mental health practitioners or academic
professionals with graduate degrees in the mental health fields. The
participants were Black women who treat the mental health needs
of other Black women. Participants answered open-ended questions
about their experiences working with Black female clients or research
participants. The four basic questions were inquiries about the
definitions of inner peace, specific challenges Black women face in
achieving inner peace, the most frequent issues that arise in sessions
with Black women, and the favorite techniques suggested for Black
female clients to achieve happiness and balance. Below I quote at
length from the paper Dr. Bell wrote summarizing her findings,
because of the significance of her conclusions.

Of the conclusion of the study, Dr. Bell wrote: "It appears that the first
step to achieving inner peace for Black women may be believing that
peace is even possible for Black women. A number of participants
had trouble themselves even identifying with the concept of true
happiness, balance, and mental health. Many Black women see peace
as a luxury for White women and as something not allowed for Black
women. Responses suggested a number of reasons for this belief.
Some Black women reason that, because the overall understanding is

that mental illness happens only to White women, then the healing modalities available are developed for, and applicable to, White women specifically. As such, achieving mental clarity, happiness, and inner peace is a status reserved for White women. Participants stated that many of their clients had built their identities around the stressors in their lives, describing themselves as 'overworked single mother' or 'unfulfilled wife' as though those were demographic box choices on the US Census. The attachment to this identity is difficult to disband, making the achievement of inner peace seemingly 'impossible.'

"Some of those who find peace 'possible' see it as a negative. Peace for some Black women seems to be associated with childhood because of the assumed freedom from responsibilities. Adults don't have 'peace,' not when they are taking care of business. The practitioner respondents suggested that many of their Black female clients viewed the notion of 'peace' as immature; a fantasy concept for people who aren't committed to their families or careers...Those uncomfortable with the very notion of finding peace admit to breaking their children out of the myth of peaceful existence because that 'isn't the real world.' For fear of raising a lazy child, and supporting the omnipresent stereotype, Black women at times attempt to make their children feel guilty for living a carefree existence... A large part of the practice of many of the Black female practitioners...is teaching Black women how to celebrate themselves."

In our conversation, Dr. Bell said, "Teaching Black women to celebrate themselves is hard. My clients come into my office with their cell phones constantly ringing. They are busy, busy, busy. They are overwhelmed with commitments, with little or no time for themselves. And even women who do yoga, who are professionally successful, ask in the middle of a session, 'Am I allowed to feel this? To say this?' They ask for permission to reveal their feelings in the middle of a session."

When I asked about the obstacles African American women face as they work to create lives of balance, Dr. Bell said, "There are so many things we carry. We carry the world on our shoulders. We carry other people's stuff and issues. We carry the expectation that we will always say yes. We carry enormous guilt. We are so hard on ourselves. We carry the guilt of those who have committed crimes against us. We carry guilt about naming Black people who have harmed us because of a misguided sense of racial loyalty. And we carry weight. A lot of it. Weight that is the literal and figurative symbolism of all those other burdens. Weight that is killing us."

The assumption that inner peace and contentment is reserved for White women stunned me. I found it frightening and tragic because I knew how the belief found expression in all manner of health crises from stroke to heart attack. For many Black women, resilience means constant physical and emotional endurance. The optimism, the sense that life is and should be ever-unfolding, an experience that offers respite as well as toil and trouble, is beyond their reach and, most importantly, beyond their imagination.

The bottled-up rage, the stunted sense of life's possibilities, course through their bodies like a poison that, even when it erupts in a health crisis, may be ignored, because that's what Strong Black Women do.

Yet, when I discussed the results of this study with a group of women, each of them, myself included, recalled actions, decisions, thoughts that revealed that we had often reflexively refused to accept help, or make self-care a priority, because as Black women we didn't have the time, couldn't make the time, or saw taking a time-out, or giving responsibility to others, as shirking our duty. We would never have expressed it in these words, but, like the women in that study, we too felt "that was a White woman thing."

One woman in the group remembered, "Several years ago, I was working for a prominent nonprofit and a White female colleague was diagnosed with a throat tumor. She decided, although it was not cancerous and her doctor told her no procedures were yet needed and that he would simply keep her under observation, to take time off from her job to lessen the stress of her life and do as much as she could to possibly heal. I was astonished. In her situation, I could have afforded to do the same thing, but it never would have occurred to me, never in a million years back then, to care that much about my health. And I concluded she was a privileged White woman who because of that could do something I couldn't. When I look back, I realize that it's not that I couldn't have done what she did. I just couldn't have imagined it."

This conversation took place three days after the death of George Floyd, a Black man murdered in Minneapolis during an arrest after a White officer pinned the handcuffed Floyd to the ground and held his knee on his neck for eight minutes and forty-six seconds. This while Floyd cried repeatedly that he could not breathe. I spoke with these women amidst national protests against systemic police violence against African Americans, protests that saw unprecedented thousands of Whites join Blacks, Latinx, Asians, Native Americans, and others in cities across America. Protests that became global.

Another friend told me, "There's this unspoken feeling of dread as we wait for the next awful video assassination of a Black person, by the police or by a private White citizen, essentially for being Black. Look at the Black and brown bodies piling up disproportionately as a result of the COVID-19 pandemic. My daughter is having her first child soon, and I tell you I'm afraid the racial progress clock is being turned back just as my grandchild enters the world. How could I possibly take time out for myself? We're always in a state of emergency and we need all hands on deck."

"The Strong Black Woman began as a way to empower us," Dr. Bell said. "It said 'You can't keep us down. Whatever you throw at us, we continue to rise. We can pray and we can push for change. We can do it all. Everything and not break a sweat. Never tire. Never complain. Never cry.' But what was adaptive has become clearly maladaptive. A mentally healthy Strong Black Woman cries, and she asks for help because she knows she is stronger in community."

Lauren Carson has seen young Black girls modeling the Strong Black Woman syndrome. Dr. Kanika Bell has found that many Black women can't even imagine peace and contentment. Professor Seanna Leath, Associate Professor of Psychology at the University of Virginia, has found similar patterns among college-aged Black women. We discussed her study of African American college women aged eighteen to twenty-four attending historically White universities.

"These were young Black women, full-time students, not yet shouldering the full economic responsibilities of adulthood," she told me. "I found that they really want to embody and be the Strong Black Woman. These are young women working very hard to exceed personal and family expectations. They often cited mothers, grandmothers, and other women who had been models of selfless strength, and they said again and again, 'That's what I want to be.'"

"Many of them said they never saw their mothers cry. Or 'I knew my mother was stressed, but she never showed it.' That comment revealed that they had not had conversations about the negative impact of the masking of pain and frustration, the emotional and physical toll on those women's health. Out of the group, about one-fourth had a parent who was a counselor or who had talked with them or someone else about this aspect of the Strong Black Woman syndrome, but most had not."

Professor Leath also found that "these young women, students at White colleges preparing often to work in 'the White world' had also begun mastering self-management."

Fearful of being labeled Angry Black Women, the young women often chose not to respond to racist comments, or to what they felt were misinterpretations of Black culture and life in their classes, where they were often the only Black student. "I'd be dismissed if I got angry," one young woman said. Dr. Leath said, "The Strong Black Woman syndrome acts as an effective and powerful silencing factor." When asked if they had any safe spaces in their lives where they could express anger, few young women said they did. "It's like we're being gaslighted," one young woman said. "Like it's not legitimate for us to be angry, so you end up second-guessing yourself."

As Professor Leath and I talked, I wondered: if these relatively well-off, middle-class young Black women had yet to find ways to ensure their mental health, how did Black women with fewer economic resources and career opportunities make time for counseling and therapy? I also remembered my years teaching in a graduate creative writing program at the same kind of prestigious White university these young women attended, where, as a resource for the students in the program, I was undervalued, underutilized, and marginalized.

I did this work in an environment where nobody called me nigger, but one where female and Black students found the atmosphere in the writing workshops led by some of my White male colleagues so unwelcoming to their work that they had stories they submitted for workshop, and stories they only shared with each other. With all my big voice, and all the thousands of words I had written, I too engaged in self-management of my anger and rage. I slept poorly. I felt isolated. For years I second-guessed the extent of the racism I was experiencing, until I finally broke my silence and shared my feelings with women of color in other graduate programs who, I found, shared similar experiences of marginalization. I didn't really second-guess my experience; I just did not want to accept it. *Who would? Who can you talk to in an environment where your White colleagues think your mere presence means racism cannot possibly exist?* one friend asked.

While at this university, I lacked the supportive group of Black female fellow faculty that I had relied on at my previous school, but the love of my husband, sister-friends, family, and my writing kept me emotionally balanced even as I sometimes feared I was nearing a cliff.

"Even among an informal group of women I meet with regularly, a kind of sister circle, I see the same pattern," Professor Leath said. "We talk a lot about racist incidents and how we should respond. There's a feeling among many in the group that we have to constantly be engaged in protest and activism. If I don't do it, who will, is the question. But when we cite women like Ida B. Wells and others, I often ask myself, 'Do we always have to be in battle? Didn't Wells and other women also fight so that we could have the right to sit down? To rest?' It seems that it's so much easier for us to think about the big issues we face as a people than ourselves."

The New Age Strong Black Woman, a definition: I propose that we take the best attributes of the Strong Black Woman syndrome—loyalty to others, resilience, determination, confidence—and fuse those qualities with love of ourselves, listening to our bodies and minds and spirits, acting to ensure their health and well-being, and becoming willing to ask others for help and support. The New Age Strong Black Woman gives herself permission to say no and make it a one-word sentence, and makes self-care a regular part of her life.

Becoming A New Age Strong Black Woman...

> Let's talk about our health the way we gossip, the way we talk about our favorite TV show, the way we complain about our job or family members who are challenging us—easily, comfortably. Let's talk about health before we get sick. Let's get all up in the health business of our sister-friends and family. And let them get all up in our health business too. Because we love them. Because they love us. One of my dearest friends was overweight for years, and I did not know how to talk to her about how I felt her excess weight was dangerous without shaming her, without rupturing some aspect of our decades-old friendship. She has now gotten healthy and has lost weight. But the weight loss was a response to a major wake-up call. During a routine visit for a checkup, which she had not had in several years, my friend learned that without knowing it, she was living in the heart attack and stroke zone. Her doctor put her on a regimen of blood pressure medications that have helped her maintain a healthy blood pressure. She became more active, and has since lost weight and is now much more health-conscious.

If I wanted to talk to an overweight friend today, I would not talk about her weight. I would talk about her health. I'd have a conversation about my last annual checkup, my last doctor's visit, and ask her about her health. How is your health? A simple question that can open possibilities for discussion and sharing. Because we don't talk about health until we are sick, we don't get practice in making health a subject associated with life rather than death, well-being rather than illness. Let's detoxify conversations about our health needs and desires. Let's also recognize that, for women who have been unhealthy for years, it will take time to even think about and embrace the idea of getting healthy. Let your friends know that you support their process no matter how long it takes. Talk about your health often with your children, your spouse, your family. Don't allow conversations about good health to remain taboo. As my friend's story illustrates, concern about our health can't be shelved or put off. My friend was lucky her wake-up call didn't involve a heart attack or a stroke.

Through the Fire

*"We must embrace pain then burn
it as fuel for the journey"*

—Kenji Miyazawa, poet

I am making this narrative journey with my sisters. It never occurred to me to make it alone. They are with me as I cross borders, step into the minefield, stand in the harsh light of calling out and calling on the conundrum of the Strong Black Woman syndrome. I asked and searched for Black women's stories. Stories untold, unheralded. Stories hibernating. Stories that are a reflection of what we are—precious, tender, fragile. Worth fighting for. Stories of our glory and our loss.

How do you hurt? Where do you hurt? How does your hurt feel? When was the last time someone who wasn't a doctor asked you that? What does your healing sound like? What is it made of? Do you create it alone, or are there other hands holding yours? When were you last praised? When did you last rejoice? Can you rejoice in yourself? By yourself? What does it mean to you to be a Strong Black Woman? I know what I know about me. Sort of. Sometimes. I know my shifting sands. But now that I am here, now that I have set sail, I cannot launch alone. My sisters and their stories are necessary and I cannot navigate the murky waters of this exploration without them. This narrative, these pages, these words, are communal property. This is a house of stories designed to give us shelter.

Florence

"My mother was not someone who tried to be a Strong Black Woman. I was one of three children raised by a single mother and there wasn't a day that I wasn't aware of how hard my mother struggled to do that that job well. My father left us when my brothers and I were very young. It just felt like his absence was this gaping hole in all our lives. We weren't poor. My mother had what would be considered a good job with local government. But trying to handle, to raise three children alone was a source of pain and trauma for her. Her husband, our father, was gone. He left and didn't look back. She never found out until many years later where he went. Looking back now I can see that in a way every day was a day of grieving for her. She'd cry sometimes and complain about the pressure she was under. How hard it all was, trying to do this really big job. And do it alone. So she was strong enough to show weakness, that's the kind of Strong Black Woman my mother was. Maybe that's why I didn't have a problem going into therapy when I needed to.

"After law school I got a job with a big firm in Chicago as one of scores of associates. The environment was brutal. There was the insane workload and the institutional racism in an environment where all the White folks considered themselves liberal. This was back in the late seventies, back when there weren't terms like microaggression, when we just called it what it was, plain old racism. I remember I had a Black woman mentor at another firm, and she told me how often in meetings and interactions with her White colleagues she simply felt invisible. How they had perfected making her feel like she wasn't even there. I didn't know what to say to her because it sounded like she was living my life. She eventually had a stroke. By year two at the firm, I was having horrible stomach problems which my doctor diagnosed as the beginnings of an ulcer. She immediately told me to see a therapist to find out why the stress I was under was showing up in my body like that.

"I got into therapy, and it helped. But in all honesty, I had to go through two Black women therapists to find the right one. Just because the therapist is Black, that's no guarantee. Finding a good therapist, the one that speaks to you and your soul, takes time. One thing I learned is that I was in the law for the status and money and some other wrong reasons. I'd squashed my love of art and design. I changed my career and that radically improved my life. Over the years, I've been on the couch at moments of crisis. But I never stayed too long. Just long enough to get the tools I needed to do the work. *You* have to do the work, whatever that means for you. The 'work' I've done on myself is made up of a lot of things. I was into Buddhism for a while and I still meditate. Groups have been absolutely essential for me, the group of women artists I have dinner with a couple of times a year, a progressive political group I am part of. And I have a wide circle of friends. This is my support system, and it's like an interconnected family. The book *The Four Agreements* had a powerful effect on me. It helped me get out of my own head and realize that not everything, really, is about me. But I feel like every day I learn a little more about how to be me. And that's pretty exciting. And it's always, always a surprise."

Yvonne

Yvonne lost her mother, found her father (hidden in plain sight), and has learned and is still learning how to overcome and "become." At twenty-two, Yvonne has been in some form of counseling or therapy, at various times, since she was fifteen. In a society where the mantra is that everything worth anything is fast and easy, Yvonne has found that growing up is slow and hard. Therapy and counseling are where she catches her breath, where she can be uncertain, where there is time and space to reacquaint herself with who she is and get an introduction to who she can be. She is quiet, introverted, and thoughtful. My questions and probing are patiently borne. Yvonne seems to take in each inquiry like a small meal that she digests slowly. Her answers are carefully considered, as precise as she can make them. And because of that, I feel that every answer is honest. Every answer is true.

Depression. Anxiety. They have haunted the margins of Yvonne's life. Her mother, she says, "worked a lot." As a registered nurse working two jobs, a wife, and mother to three children, her plate was full. There was the stress of a marriage in which, Yvonne says, "I saw my parents argue, heard the whispers through the bedroom walls. Arguments over the recurring problems, over and over, problems that never seemed to get solved." Her natural tendency to shelter her emotions was reinforced. "It was ingrained in me not to talk back to adults. There wasn't much open conversation with my mother, and I didn't feel I could bring problems to her. Whatever was bothering me, I had to live with it and move on. Like when my parents went through a rough patch, I felt like my mother was the one really suffering. She stuck it out. She put the family first."

Then one night, coming home from one of her two jobs, Yvonne's mother's car veered off the road and hit a tree. She was killed instantly. All evidence pointed to driver fatigue as the cause of the fatal crash. But as was now habit, no one talked about that at all.

Then her father did something unexpected. Despite his own history of depression, or maybe because of it, or because his wife's death had opened something in him that until then had been sealed, he got the family into grief counseling.

Yvonne's mother had been omnipresent, omniscient even, working those two jobs, running the household. Now her father was the only parent Yvonne and her brothers had left. The father that she mostly talked to as he drove her to school, the father that she had never felt she really knew, *that father* stepped out of the shadows. There were individual and group sessions with the counselor. "I don't remember much meaningful conversation with my father until my mom died. In therapy, he opened up. I learned so much about him. About how he has struggled with depression, depression that I couldn't see. He wasn't good at providing emotional support until then. I guess because he'd always needed so much himself." In what was left of a family where silence and distance was the norm, her father had with his actions told his children that he loved them.

When Yvonne transferred to a large public high school, from the small Christian academy she had attended; when she enrolled in a White university in Boston and "felt anxious because I was this very quiet, Black person on a nearly all-White campus and afraid to speak up in class"; when her supervisor on her first full-time job after college made her feel devalued; at all these passage points, she actively sought counseling. She knew there were some things she couldn't do alone. And conquering her deepest fears was one of them. She found her friends could only take her so far.

Her life has been a battle. In a world that seems made for the loud, the opinionated, and the overconfident, how would the depth of her unique quiet wisdom, her talents, ever be heard? As a young woman standing literally on the cusp of adulthood, these are crucial, life-defining questions that Yvonne has explored. Now she has a better sense of balance, she says. What she values most right now, she tells me, is that she is learning how to create a relationship with her father. The father who had once seemed to be an illusion is now a solid, enduring presence in her life. Being a parent. Being a child. No way around it, there are always more questions than answers. But Yvonne is patient; she is willing to do whatever it takes. To wait. And to ask. And to listen.

Sara

"I learned how to be a strong Black woman from a strong White woman. My mother was White, and I was abandoned by her and became a ward of the state of Pennsylvania. I was considered difficult to place, but my parents, a White couple living in Bucks County, Pennsylvania, a suburb of Philly, adopted me and my brother, who's Native American but doesn't really identify that way. My teenaged mother abandoned me in the hospital, so I was a ward of the state until I was adopted. My brother and I were legally adopted together through a social worker from the state's welfare department. My adoptive mother grew up on a farm, so she was familiar with hardship and weathering storms. Her motto was, if you feel bad, just keep on moving. So I learned to be strong from her, and then I learned to be strong on my own. I became at an early age my own kind of Strong Black woman. Bucks County, despite being not far from Philly, was then and still is a virulently racist place. I mean KKK and Neo-Nazi racist. I mean like I had to leave places because people were shouting nigger at me.

"School was almost totally White. I got punished for infractions I never committed by being shut in a closet all day. It went like this: if something was stolen, maybe in a part of the school I had not been in, they came and got me and searched my bookbag. When the object wasn't found and I tried to defend myself, then I'd get written up for insubordination, and get put in the storage closet. Teachers would

say to my face that they didn't know what to do with me. They let me
know that the closet punishment was devised just for me. I was told,
'We don't need you here, you'll never amount to anything, so why does
it matter what we do to you?' My parents were in denial and didn't
want to talk about the racism around us, and what I experienced. That
was their defense mechanism. I was terribly isolated and alone. So I got
into drugs. Staying high helped me cope.

"I was bright, curious, eager to learn, but all that got shut down.
Somehow, after high school I got into Temple University in Philly.
At Temple I discovered Black literature and the poet Sonia Sanchez,
a professor in the English Department. Those two things saved my
life. Reading James Baldwin, and all the other Black writers, I realized
that I belonged to a people who had walked tall despite oppression.
Sometimes, sitting in the library, those books brought me to tears
because I had found my home. Those stories taught me racism wasn't
a personal vendetta against me, it was historical, it was cultural.
I realized that enduring all that had happened to me, the actions
against me at school and the silence of my parents, was me standing
in the river of history, getting dunked. But Giovanni, and Jordan
and Lorde and Walker, showed me that I had not gone down to stay
down forever.

"I was still getting high, cause that's what I did. That's how I survived.
But I just latched onto Professor Sanchez. I took all her classes. And
one day she asked me the question that, if you hear it at the right
moment, changes your life. She asked what I was going to do with
myself. I just blurted out, 'I want to do what you do.' She didn't laugh
at me. She just told me that, in order to do what she did, I'd have to
go to Howard University for graduate school. I was burnt out, but at
the same time inspired, and I applied for Howard's Black Literature
Program and got in because of her shepherding. And that was when

I finally got clear, woke up, and asked myself what Sonia had asked me, what was I going to do? What was I going to do with a life that I didn't feel anymore that I had to run from, but a life that I could hold in my hands?

"So now I had this life, this real life that was staring me in the face. And I could see it up close, see it for real, because I stopped using drugs. But without the drugs I was all rage. If somebody pissed me off, I got physical immediately. My anger drove away a boyfriend and almost destroyed friendships. It was crazy, but it was kind of exhilarating. I had tamped down the anger I felt for so long, masked it with the drugs, that once I started feeling the anger and expressing it, I almost couldn't stop. I had girlfriends who were worried about me and urged me to get therapy because I clearly had anger management problems. The most important thing I learned in therapy is what had happened to me growing up. It's like I had been in a war. It had felt like a war against me, but no one would ever use that word. I had been traumatized and I wasn't just angry, I had post-traumatic stress disorder. All that seems far away and yet it's all right here with me. I'm married now and have a son. Because I had to be so strong, I realize that a part of me never respected people who couldn't handle things. I tend to take on a lot out of habit, to shoulder things and then end up feeling burdened.

"I'm a workaholic, but there are so many life rafts now, my husband, my son, my writing and teaching, martial arts, and plain old prayer gets me through more days than I can count. Growing up in a mostly White community, I feel that Black folk are mentally healthier than White suburban communities like the one I grew up in. In White suburban communities, people don't talk about problems. There's a communal charade that everything is fine, that their manicured lawns and good manners mean that nobody's getting molested or being beaten by their husbands. Sanctions against talking about negative things are strong. But since I defected from Bucks County in the late '80s, I've never ceased to be impressed by how Black folk are willing to discuss things that aren't 'happy.' We deserve credit, at least for that."

Jamie

The story of a family torn apart by alcoholism is one that in some ways we all know. Fifteen million Americans struggle with the disease. Alcoholics are family members, friends, spouses, coworkers. We've seen the wreckage close up, felt helpless watching from afar the turmoil alcoholism inflicts. And we've felt guilt and impotence at our inability to rescue or protect the children of alcoholic parents.

We know the story, or think we do. The instability and unpredictability of life in the home of an alcoholic. Parents who morph into monsters. Children unable to be children because of the cruel role reversal their home life requires. Children who become decision-makers, counselors to parents, and learn to survive by masking their feelings.

But the trauma that flourishes in the home of the alcoholic, while wounding children, can conversely produce a deep well of traits that, when combined with treatment for their emotional scars, can bode well for success later in life. Problem-solving, quick thinking, taking on responsibility, negotiating outcomes. All these adaptations are acquired at a steep price. A price that, down the line, will have to be reckoned with.

Jamie grew up in a home with an alcoholic father who physically abused her mother. The home was a danger zone of competing, contradictory messages and demands. There was her father, whose alcoholic rages too often turned into violent attacks on her mother. Not until she was an adult did Jamie learn that her father had been abandoned by his parents and raised in an abusive environment by family members. These were the unseen, secret wounds he carried. Still, her father grew up, found a steady job, and, as Jamie said, "when they were just kids" he and her mother met, fell in love, and married. Her father sought the stability he'd never known and worked to build a white-picket-fence life for his family.

Parents and extended family had failed him, but he believed in God. Fiercely. There was power and redemption in faith, he felt, so with his wife, his son and daughter, come every Sunday, they were in church. Then there was her mother, the stable bedrock who suffered kidney failure for years before a successful kidney transplant.

As the oldest child, Jamie was doctor, nurse, therapist, counselor, protector of her younger brother, as the family roiled from one crisis to another. "I counseled my dad when he was sobbing drunk. Took my mom to the emergency room dozens of times when her kidneys were failing. Everybody leaned on me." They all leaned on her because Jamie had called on the love of her family, and survival instincts to be all things to everybody. And this was a home where, despite it all, everyone believed.

"No doubt, we were jacked up. We were a mess. But our church was where we all came together no matter what. I remember when I was ten years old, one Sunday, I went up to the sanctuary and a woman prayed over me. She affirmed my purpose and what God had in store for me, I'll never forget that. The memory of that woman's hands kept pushing me through everything. That and the family prayer line that my mother's side of the family set up and that I am still a part of. My own faith. My mother's faith. All of that got me through everything."

And everything included, while in college, being the family breadwinner, using her scholarship money to buy food and pay household bills. Everything included watching her parent's thirty-six-year marriage end, but because endings are rarely neat, seeing bitterness and distance and quarrels still erupt.

"Because by then I was deeply into the superwoman, the Strong Black Woman syndrome, all of this was my burden to carry," Jamie said. But at nineteen she took the first of many steps to lay her burden down, by going to counseling for adult children of alcoholics. "Prayer led me to counseling. All my life I had been told not to share our business. But prayer helped me realize it was okay to seek professional counseling outside the church." She had found faith to endure and overcome in church, but in group counseling she could hear and see through the din and the fog of her life at home. She began to put the pieces together like a puzzle. Her father told her, "Stand up for yourself, don't let White people keep you down." But that warning was followed by the accusation that she talked too much and had a "smart mouth." Her mother said, "Be a proud Black woman. Be strong. I love you. But don't tell anybody our business. Tell me what you feel. But I need you. You can handle this. You are the first one I call. The one I can always depend on."

Jamie was crumbling beneath the burden, but in group therapy, that was one place where she could be herself, something she was still discovering. In the midst of this turmoil and pain, she had what she would call the first honest conversation she had ever had with her parents. "I told them I can't carry you. I can't carry my anger. I can't carry my hurt." She set boundaries and put herself first. "I wasn't protected as a child, but now I was ready to protect myself. I told them, I love you mom, I love you dad, but I release you. I choose me." And in choosing herself, she could see herself as the woman she now made time and space to become, a journalist, an activist for women's rights, and, she will always say, "a believer." Her father stopped drinking, just stopped cold turkey. But Jamie says, "He's deep in the church, deep in his faith, but still full of anger."

Because she had witnessed her parents regularly running out of words or falling back on words that maimed, Jamie values, most of all in her journey, that she now knows how to communicate effectively. "That is what I wanted more than anything," she told me. Prayer, therapy, her training as a journalist, working on a PhD, her faith in herself and her family, all of that helped her create a vocabulary for her life, a life that she says as a child she could never have imagined. "And the biggest surprise of all," she tells me, "is that I have a healthy, respectful, and loving relationship with a Black man. We've been together four years, and I just never saw that happening for me." Jamie says, "I wouldn't be here if not for my faith in Jesus, and my Jesus is a revolutionary, an activist." Jamie did not "pray it away." Prayer became a conduit to all the things and people that helped her to fulfill the affirmation of the woman who laid hands on her when she was ten years old. That woman knew back then that Jamie would indeed walk through the fire to the other side.

Shelley

"My journey to achieve and maintain mental health is affected by both my mother and my father. By what happened to my dad and the way that my mother handled it. My father was bipolar and schizophrenic. As a child, all I knew was that there were times when daddy was well and times when he was so sick that he had to leave us and go to the hospital, sometimes for as long as a month. My dad sold electronics, TVs, and radios at Sears. I loved him and never felt afraid of him. I just knew that sometimes he was at home, not working, and he seemed really sad. Sometimes he was working, and things seemed normal, and at other times he was gone. My mother told me that he had a sickness that you couldn't see.

"Looking back, I remember going to a friend's house once, I was pretty young, maybe five or six. I went into the kitchen and saw a lot of knives on the counter, and I realized then that I never saw knives at our house. I thought not having knives in the house was normal, the way everyone lived, but that day I realized it wasn't. Years later I learned that my mother had buried all our knives in the backyard to keep them from my father.

"It could not have been easy for my mother. She had to try to support my father emotionally while being the major breadwinner. She was a high school teacher and had a small tutoring business on the side. She paid the bills, attended PTA meetings, kept the house and family running. She cried a lot. She was angry a lot. I never felt unsafe around my dad, but he could have been violent with my mother. Clearly, if she hid the knives, she was afraid he might harm himself or someone else.

"When I was seven, my parents divorced. It happened during one of my father's hospitalizations. That day my mother woke me and my sister up and we went to school. After school, she picked us up and took us to our grandmother's house. She had packed up all our clothes, our toys, everything, and moved it to her mother's house. And just like that, we had a new life. One minute I had a home with my dad, the next minute I didn't. I loved my dad so much. That day changed the way I felt about my mother. In my mind she was the person who took me away from my dad. I've felt that loss all my life.

"For my mom, leaving my dad didn't mean that she cried less or that she was less sad. Despite the tears and the sadness, she got really involved in our church, she volunteered a lot. She volunteered for everything and the church became her escape. I think in the church she felt valued and important. The church was her safety valve.

"We were never told anything really about my dad's illness, and now we weren't being told much about why we had left my dad. Sometimes he visited us, but the visits were awful. There was so much tension. I was conflicted because I loved my dad and I wanted to love him, but because we'd left him, I felt that I couldn't love him. Living with my grandmother, I remember any time I looked at a picture of him or saw him in films of us as a family, my grandmother badmouthed my father. So I felt like I had to censor memories of him. Pretty soon he visited us less and less, and when I was in the fourth grade, he stopped visiting at all. It felt like he just disappeared. He was erased in our family, and it was an unspoken rule that we didn't talk about him. If I mentioned my dad, my mother would start crying. Back then her tears didn't move me, because I hated her because she'd separated me from my father, and I was crying tears of my own. But now I know she was grieving.

"From childhood I have suffered with anxiety and depression, but I was absolutely terrified of telling anyone how I felt because I was afraid that if I did, that would mean I was like my dad. I felt that I'd be erased from the family if I was honest about my emotions, so I suffered in silence for a long time.

"By the time I was in fifth grade, a year after my parents divorced, I had bottled up my emotions so much that the only way I could express any feelings was by exploding, blowing up. Our house was full of stress and tension. I felt abandoned by my father, and silenced by my family. My mother took me to a therapist, and I did open up. It helped a little. But it was years before I got a formal diagnosis of depression.

"Recently I was with some friends from college and we were reminiscing, and I had one version of those days and they had another. They told me what they remembered was me sleeping all the time. I'd go to class, study, then go to my dorm room and get in the bed and sleep. I'd buried memories of how much I wanted to escape my life. They were right. I slept. A lot. I had friends but no boyfriend, because there was the constant fear that I'd pick someone like my dad. I'd sabotage relationships, end them for no apparent reason, so that couldn't happen.

"The anxiety and the depression continued after college. Finally, it all came to a head. I was twenty-nine years old, crying all the time. Sleeping excessively. My energy felt low, heavy. I had trouble sleeping. I was quickly becoming addicted to a liquid nighttime over-the-counter medicine for insomnia. Night after night, I drank the stuff. My soul felt unsettled. I felt miserable and so alone. I wanted help. I wanted to tell someone about being depressed all the time, but there was this argument raging in my head. 'What will happen if I tell the truth? Will I be erased like my dad?' Finally, one night, just before I was getting ready to sip the medicine, a voice, I can only call it God, told me to go to therapy, told me I had nothing to fear. Told me it would be alright. I was so disenchanted by how I saw my mother use the church to run from her problems that I hadn't been inside a church in fourteen years. But God or one of His angels found me anyway.

"The first therapist immediately wanted to put me on drugs that I didn't feel I needed. The second therapist felt I would probably only need one visit. The third therapist, she just had this calm, this soothing energy, and I started crying the moment I sat down in the chair. She handed me a tissue and I just felt completely safe with her. I saw her twice a week for two years, and she was excellent at helping me unpack everything I had buried from the age of seven to thirty-two.

"She was the first person to name what I was feeling. One of the tools she taught me was how to log into my feelings. On a nightly basis, I'd write in a journal how I felt that day. Writing my feelings down on paper centered me. It really helped with my anxiety and helped me process all those feelings. At first, I felt shame about seeing a therapist, but then I began talking about it openly with friends. I talked about it casually, like it was no big thing, and soon several friends told me they too wanted to get help.

"It felt really empowering to have that impact on their lives. I told them that, just like them, I was falling apart on the inside and trying to hold it together. Therapy helped me stop being so angry with my mother. Our relationship is still challenging, but I no longer see her as the enemy. I see her as a victim, like we all were. As for my dad, I still haven't been able to reach out to him. To overcome all the fear and negativity I learned to associate with him and his mental illness. Not yet. But maybe someday."

Queen

"Many people in my life find it very hard to believe that I had a mental breakdown. After all, I was the strong friend. And the one in my family that everyone relied on. I had reached a peak…or so it seemed. I'd just finished up a highly coveted internship in the Obama White House and had managed to secure a job with the federal government right out of college. I was living in a new city and was excited about the possibilities that lay ahead for my career. To others, at that time, my life seemed close to perfect. But behind the excitement of it all, I was slowly falling into a funk. I call it a funk because, back then, I didn't know what it was. In December of that year, a doctor would give my funk a name: temporary psychosis with acute mania.

"We'd had a beautiful Christmas dinner. The next day, I became overwhelmed with thoughts that everyone around me was disappointed in me and wanted to harm me. I was surrounded by my closest loved ones, but in a fit of extreme paranoia, I yelled at them. I accused them of judging me; I kicked and screamed as they attempted to put me in a car. That day turned into a weeklong stay in a mental health facility, where I went through a cycle of taking medications with long names, sleeping for hours on end only to wake up fighting extreme panic attacks. Attendants would deliver more medication, I'd fall asleep, and the cycle would repeat. When I finally snapped back to some sense of normalcy, I sat in silence for days trying to understand what could have possibly brought me to this moment. I know now that I felt weighed down by more things than any one person should have to carry alone.

"Despite all of the positive things going on in my life at the time, I couldn't seem to stop myself from honing in on the negatives. Instead of focusing on the great friendship I'd built with the guy I was dating, I'd spend hours stressing over whether our long-distance relationship would last. My work, if not always exciting, was certainly a bridge to a promising career. Yet, on most days, I felt taking the job had been the biggest mistake of my life. And more than anything, I felt alone.

"I was living in a city where the only people I knew were my coworkers, and all of the people I loved were hundreds of miles away, including my then four-year-old daughter. When I couldn't afford the high rent in the new city in addition to the cost of childcare, I was forced to leave my daughter in my hometown with my mother. For several months, I had to take a four-hour bus ride to see them every weekend. Even when I could afford to bring my daughter to live with me several months later, I still felt sad because I missed everyone else. I missed my siblings, I missed my friends, and I missed my church.

"My mother was a strong, enduring Black woman. What I learned from watching her work hard and basically give herself away was that my value was determined by how much I could help other people. I had to be useful, productive. I've often felt that Black women benefit the least from all the hard work we do. But I got the message, and because of what I learned at home and because of racism and the need to be twice as good at anything I did, it was never enough for me to be good. I had to be the best. In some instances, on jobs I've been shamed, criticized by others because I worked so hard. But that drive for excellence is just ingrained in me.

"My mother married twice and divorced twice. There were seven of us children in our blended family. We were a big family and I was the second child. My older sister attended LaSalle University in Philadelphia. It had a major impact on me that I saw my big sister do that, so I followed her lead. But in the middle of my sophomore year, I had a tuition balance I couldn't pay. I reasoned that my only option was to take a semester off, save some money, and come back the following semester. That semester turned into a six-year break. During those six years I went from being a waitress, saving tips for school, to being an administrative assistant at a local finance company with no clear plans for returning to college. I got pregnant, and planning for motherhood changed everything. It changed my life. I realized I had to go back to college. I went back to LaSalle, finished, and got my bachelor's degree.

"But there's a backstory. Because my mother went through a long period of depression when we were younger, the older children, my sister and I, basically raised the younger children in the family. Because of my take-charge nature, over time, I became the child that everyone depended on, came to for answers when they were in crisis, when they needed money, when they needed a place to live. My mother would ask totally unreasonable things of me, or ask my siblings to ask me for her. And for a long time, I didn't know how to not solve their problems for them. All I knew how to do was say yes. My older sister could say no and established boundaries that I couldn't.

"I had the breakdown at what should have been a high point in my life. I'd completed college, interned at the White House, and was a media specialist for the Department of the Interior. But I cracked. I just didn't know anyone who had had that experience, so in the early days after the breakdown I was still confused about what had happened to me. I started learning more about mental health during my time as a reporter at NBC10 in Philly, and later I made some new friends through other jobs, and they all talked so openly about going to therapy or needing therapy that it helped me see it as something that might be helpful. But really, the hospital wasn't helpful at all. The discharge paperwork said temporary psychosis with acute mania. I stared at those words for two weeks and thought it meant I was crazy.

"The hospital recommended I follow up with a therapist in a week and provided a number for a therapist, but therapy just wasn't a thing that you did in my family. So I didn't know how it would be helpful and I didn't go. There was also this notion I grew up with that you don't tell strangers your business. My mother often said, 'Don't let them put anything bad about you on record. They will pull it back up later to hurt you.' I know there is some truth to her warning, but all of that probably contributed to me trying to just get back to normal on my own. I've since learned anxiety and mania may run in the family, as both my mother and father have developed some paranoia issues that they deny and disregard, and they also minimized the reality of one of my younger brothers's two breakdowns. All of that made me want to learn how to manage what I was feeling. What I now know is I definitely have anxiety, and when it gets bad, I have panic attacks. And whether they call it that or not, several others in my family probably have that too.

"After my breakdown, my mother got a huge settlement from a traffic accident she had been in several years earlier that had contributed to her depression and inability to work. It was a lot of money, and my generous big-hearted mother took care of everyone in the family, including me. But in two years the money was gone, and I was back to being the family anchor.

"I kept moving up in my career, in public relations, communication, and journalism. The higher up I moved, the more needy my family became. My sister and I are the only ones who went to college. The only ones with stable careers. And since my sister could and would say no, everyone came to me. A couple of years later I was building a solid, satisfying relationship with a new man, building a life. I didn't want family living with me anymore, taking for granted that I would be the family ATM, minister, or therapist. I had my second child, a son, and more and more I began feeling I had to have a life of my own. I began feeling depleted emotionally. One day when my sister, who was a homeless street musician, showed up at our apartment asking if she and her boyfriend could take a shower, my boyfriend got really protective of me, and our space. We had a terrible argument, my sister and [me]. My mother called and took my sister's side. I finally found the courage to say, 'I simply do not want anyone living with me anymore.' We didn't speak for months. Then I finally found the courage to go into therapy. The burden was just too much for me.

"The therapist helped me understand so much about myself. My philosophy was that I'm only okay if my family is okay. And since my family was always in crisis, I was never okay. I was always on call for any emergency. She asked me why I felt it was my responsibility to make my family members happy. She told me I could love them, but I didn't have to literally carry my family on my back. And she told me that the word *no* could be a complete sentence, and that I didn't have to explain why I said it. I'm still learning to own my yeses and my nos. I realized I was a control freak. Like a typical Strong Black Woman, I felt if I don't fix it, it won't get fixed. Now I give my family time and space to figure out their own answers and solutions. My therapist walked me through what triggered the breakdown so I could take action to defeat anxiety, the kind that made me crash and burn. I'm in a good place now, for the first time in my life saying unequivocally yes to myself."

Black families are buffeted and attacked by an array of forces beyond their control. Forces that persist in the face of patriotism, working twice as hard, political activism, faith in God. Because our families are so enduring and yet so fragile, Black women are haunted by the question and dilemma: how to love our families and not be swallowed whole by their needs. If we can't meet their needs, if we offer tough love, there is the fear that because they are Black in America, they are more vulnerable to being ensnared by disaster.

Yet we have to ask and require that our families love us as we love them. Give to us as we give to them Our families need to ask us, "What can I do for you?" Teach your family to respect your need for time-outs, retreats, down time, me time, and that therapy is an option, not a taboo. Families are only as strong as each individual member. Black women must love their families enough to love themselves.

Becoming A New Age Strong Black Woman...

The women who bravely shared with me their stories of overcoming trauma told me stories that are uplifting and inspiring. Black women are healing and holding on to the best parts of themselves everywhere. Every day. I was impressed by the complexity and power, and faithfulness, of their journeys. They used every tool available to heal. Therapy. Prayer. Meditation. Patience. Running. Forgiveness. Love. Black women are powerful believers. Believers in an unseen power that is benevolent. We have seen this faith at work in our lives. Our mothers and grandmothers have passed down accounts of how they have been delivered. And they and we are delivering ourselves. There is a new world coming, and we can design it. We can live in it.

The Reimagined History of My Heart: of Harriet, of Rosa, of Fannie Lou, of Patrisse

Quiet as it's kept, the Strong Black Woman syndrome is an invisible superpower that explains Black women's extraordinary leadership genius. We lead. We blaze new trails. That's what we do. I am so proud to be a Black woman. But as we lift up ourselves and the race, and the world, what price do we pay?

Harriet

I was called many things. Araminta. Harriet. Slave. Nigger. Useless. Fugitive. Abolitionist. Spy. General. Moses. But I'm the only one who knew my name. I was a girl-child and then I was a woman. And I was always free. That's how the Lord made me. During all my ninety-three years, everybody was always calling me something, giving me a name. Names that was a curse. Names I earned.

I just kept my peace and listened to what they said about me. What they thought they knew. About the guns I carried. The people I brought to freedom. The soldiers I led into battle. But the name that I knew was mine, that I made with my own life and living, was Woman. If I was to have the name I really wanted, it would've been just that, Woman. First name, Woman. Last name, Free.

I fought like a woman. I loved like a woman. And it was love that set me running North and then back South and then to fight for freedom, and then into what they called peace. Love. That was what sharpened my sword. That was the fire in my belly. I loved myself, my beaten and bruised and half-starved self, and my beaten and bruised and half-starved kin. Loved us all like I love God. A woman in love is a mighty force on this earth. They couldn't keep me down cause love kept pickin' me up. I disobeyed the laws of slavery and obeyed the laws of love. The kinda love driving me wasn't no dainty thing. It was all the power of heaven and even hell, working together to make the most beautiful thing I could think of, to see my family, my people free. To destroy slavery, one man, one woman, one child at a time.

There's things I saw that once I seen 'em they never left my mind. And I see 'em sunrise, and sunset. The faces of the Whites who whipped me like a mule, beat me the way they wouldn't even beat a horse, and never got tired of hatin' me. That iron weight that hit me in the head busted my head to kingdom come. That iron weight landed on me, but it lifted me too. Lifted me to a place and a pain I knew till the day I died. I'd fall out, just like I was dead, then come awake. My head was filled with the sound of a buzz saw, all noise and confusion. I say it lifted me cause after that, the visions come. Visions from God and Mary and Jesus and Joseph. Visions that took my hand and led me on. They broke me like a split tree trunk, but the splinters made me whole.

The visions were there in my head right beside my name, my real name. Woman. Free. There were other visions too. You can't never stop seeing what you see when you lead men into battle into an army raised up against you. I was the first woman to do that. It was the Civil War, June 1863, when I guided Colonel James Montgomery and his colored soldiers up the Combahee River. We sent the Confederates scrambling and ended up setting free seven hundred of my people who had been enslaved. Still, all the praying I did ain't never yet taken away the faces of colored men in blue uniforms dying to be free. Dying with their faces shot off, or begging for help they knew wasn't gonna come, or seeing a field that had once growed corn or cotton now filled with the bodies of dead men, colored and White. After a battle, watching pigs rooting through that field and eating what was left of them men, whether they was dead or alive. I dreamed about all that. And I couldn't tell nobody about them dreams cause anybody I'd tell, if they'd been in that war, I know they probably had a dream even worse than mine.

Sometimes I could make them faces go away when I remembered the face of my first husband, John Tubman. When I could see all the love that man had for me, see it shining on his face. He was a free man and he never saw me as no slave. He coulda lost me anytime. I coulda been sold to get a new horse, a dress, or a new parcel of land. Our children wouldn'a been his. I wasn't his. But he loved me free. That's love doing battle. Oh, and when I got my freedom, took it for myself, and I come back South for him and he didn't want to come with me. I never knew I had a heart till then. Hadn't felt my heartbeat, not really, till it broke when he said he wouldn't come back North with me. That broke me worse than the whipping that left my back all scarred up. But my family, my mama, my papa, other family, and others come with me to freedom in all the trips I made back South.

But love don't wait, and it don't ask permission. Love wants to be used and used all up. So after the war and being called "General," I moved to Auburn, New York. I married Nelson Davis, a colored man who'd fought in the war. A colored man who fought for his freedom and lived to see it. He was twenty-two years younger than me. But that didn't matter. I'd always felt real old, and always been real young. He'd seen the same hell I'd seen, so sometimes we could just know what the other one was thinking. We found a peace. We made a peace. But still, sometimes I'd cry cause of the stories my body told. If you looked at my back, my arms, my legs, you could see the whole terrible history of my people. But my body loved Nelson like a woman, and he held me like a man. He held me like I was precious and strong and trembling. I held him like he was all them things too.

Lord never see fit to give me a child of my own. But all around me wasn't nothing but orphans and children needing love. So we adopted a baby girl we named Gertie. I'd been almost everything you could think of, and now I was a mother.

God put life on my shoulders. Raised me from the dead over and over. I wasn't so strong. Whatever strength I had He give me. I got called. I heard the trumpets. I got called. And I couldn't say no.

Rosa

This is how you remember me: The tired seamstress who refused to give up her seat, sparking the Montgomery Bus Boycott of 1955. Prim. Proper. Even during the second arrest, when the newspapers took a photograph of me being fingerprinted, that's how I appeared. Prim. Proper. Respectable. A photograph that went all around the world. That day I was arrested with eighty-nine others, including Dr. Martin Luther King Jr.

I'd been waiting for a long time to refuse to give up my seat. Give up my seat and join all the Negro women who refused to give up their seats before me whose names got erased. Claudette Colvin. Susie McDonald. Mary Louise Smith. Jeanetta Reese. Aurelia Browder. The thing is, nobody remembers them, but they were the plaintiffs in the suit asking the courts to declare segregation unconstitutional. Not me. I got arrested on a Thursday, charged with disorderly conduct, though I was hardly disorderly. By Monday ninety percent of the Negroes in Montgomery were boycotting the buses.

History makes of you what the people who write the books and the people who read the books decide you're gonna be. There were a lot of words written about me, but many of those words were only half true. I was polite, always tried to treat people with respect. I held my tongue. I could control my anger. But I was militant. I was strategic. If there was a word that I would choose to describe me, it would be rebel. I watched my grandfather sit on the front porch with a shotgun at night to defend his home, where I grew up, against the Ku Klux Klan. And I told him more than once that I wanted to see him kill a Kluxer. I grew up on stories about Marcus Garvey and Africa and Black people needing to have land and money and power and to able to protect themselves. I came from that, and I married into that when I married Raymond Parks, who worked with the NAACP and fought to get freedom for the Scottsboro Nine.

The only thing I was tired of that day on the bus was giving in to racism, segregation, and the oppression of my people. And I'm pretty sure that day on the bus I was still thinking about fourteen-year-old Emmett Till, like most Negroes were. He'd been killed earlier that year. I was an organizer. I was a leader in the movement. Men pretty much ran the show, gave the speeches, talked to the newspapers, but behind the scenes the women did all the work to make it happen. I was an organizer and a leader. That's who I was that day on that bus. I was secretary of the local NAACP and I did more than take notes.

Back then, being a member of the NAACP in Alabama could get you killed. It got Medgar Evers killed. The state had you under surveillance, knew who you talked to, kept records on everything you did if you were trying to destroy segregation. So I wasn't prim and proper. Prim and proper women don't have lunch during the week with Fred Gray, a Montgomery lawyer, strategizing with him when was the right time, the right moment to get the buses integrated or, if we met resistance, bring the city to its knees. I always knew my day to refuse to give up my seat would come.

Prim and proper women don't investigate the stories of Negro women raped by White men. Prim and proper women couldn't stand to hear the stories I heard, stories I knew were true because I knew how vulnerable and unprotected Negro women were in the South. I investigated the rape of Recy Taylor in Abbeville, Alabama, for the NAACP. Gang raped by six White men. Even after the men confessed, the jury refused to find them guilty.

For all that, I was never scared of White people. When a White boy pushed me when I was a little girl, I pushed him right back. My grandmother told me if I wasn't careful, I'd get lynched. I told her, "Let them lynch me." You can look at me and see the African and the White and the Native American in me. There's been things written that, of all the women who refused to give up their seat on a segregated bus to a White person, I was most well-known because I'm light-skinned. And because of that, the White public in the North would feel more sympathy for our cause. I was still a Negro and light skin didn't keep me from having to obey the laws of segregation until I decided not to. Light skin didn't keep me from getting fired from my job as a seamstress at the Montgomery Fair department store. And light skin didn't shield me from the pain of my coworkers refusing to talk to me after the boycott, calling me a troublemaker. Light skin didn't stop the hateful threatening phone calls and the hate mail that started right after my arrest and followed me wherever I lived for the rest of my life.

And I lived a long time. Raymond lost his job too, and because of the stress of the backlash against us and the isolation, we felt like we were in the wilderness. Seemed like Negroes were more scared of me than of White people.

None of the civil rights groups that we had worked for offered help. We knew we'd have a price to pay. We'd been paying it all our lives. But this price, this price was heavy, and for a while would keep getting heavier. Eventually we moved to Detroit, where I had family. Raymond had to get a license and training all over again to be a barber, and I got piecework as a seamstress. I'd always prided myself on my grace under pressure, being made of steel, and soldiering on, but all that stress and disappointment caught up with me when I developed an ulcer and a throat tumor.

I lived in two rooms with my mother and husband. We were in debt because of the medical bills. I'm telling you this because I think it's important for everybody to know how much it costs to be a hero. Even when you are willing to be one.

Jet magazine did an article that let the public know how we were living, and the NAACP paid the hospital bill. By 1961, six years after the boycott, our financial situation was better. I never let being poor stop me from activism. I joined neighborhood groups to get out the vote and to improve the schools. Then in 1965, Congressman John Conyers hired me as an assistant to work in his office. Conyers was a great man. He and I got along well because he was a rebel. Like me. Then, in a two-year period, I lost my husband, my mother, and my brother. All of them died of cancer. And you can't tell me that our struggles fighting oppression and segregation, struggling for respect and equality, didn't have something to do with all of them dying like that.

And when I died, the city buses in Montgomery and Detroit reserved their front seats with black ribbon. For two days I lay in honor in the Rotunda of the US Capitol. I was honored. But I was honored even more by what some people had said about me back in Montgomery, when I was working with the NAACP: *"Oh Miss Parks, she was the lady who held my hand when my uncle got beat up. She got my kid involved in a youth program. She was the one who came and tried to get me to register to vote."*

Fannie Lou

> *"See it's time for America to wake up and know*
> *that we're not going to tolerate—we're not begging*
> *anymore. And I'm not going to say it's not any more*
> *going to die, because I'm never sure when I leave*
> *home whether I'll get back home or not. But if I fall*
> *while I'm in Kentucky, I'll fall five feet and four inches*
> *forward for freedom and I'm not backing off."*

—Fannie Lou Hamer, from a speech made in Kentucky, 1968

I was one of the wretched of the earth. I was a sharecropper. The daughter of a sharecropper. The rich, black fertile soil of Mississippi was in my bones. If I was mute and couldn't talk, my body could tell my story. My arms would tell you how, as the youngest of nineteen children, I reached out to be held by a mother and father and brothers and sisters who sheltered and loved me. My hands would remember starting to pick cotton when I was six. My feet would tell you about the feel of rags against their skin because I didn't have no shoes. My stomach would recreate the sound of being hungry, all the time, as a way of life. Cause that's the way everybody around us was living. I had polio. My womb would whisper and shed the tears I cried when I miscarried and then got sterilized without my knowledge. And after I was beaten in the county jail for working with the Student Nonviolent Coordinating Committee, SNCC, to register voters, my body never healed. How could it? When I said I was sick and tired of being sick and tired, I was sick. I was tired.

That is the story my body would tell you. But this is my story and I'm not mute. I was more than a body. I had a will, a sense of purpose that patched my broken bones and kept resurrecting my fight, my courage, at the first sign of giving up.

My body and the spirit God gave me marched me right on into the Movement. I liked that term, the Movement. That's what we were doing. Moving out of the remains of a slave past that was still hanging on, to the promise of America. Promises made to us and never fulfilled. The American flag and the American Dream were both drenched in our blood. We moved alright, off of plantations, into voting booths, and in the end, moved into the Sheriff's office, State Legislature, Congress, and though I didn't live to see it, into the White House.

I was drawn to the young people in SNCC. I admired their fire. Their impatience. They wasn't studying nothing about going slow. We was already four hundred years late. All the anger and all my feelings about injustice and the cruelty of segregation and poverty, that I had held in for years, I got to say it in a righteous, healing way to people all over the country, raising money for SNCC.

One day there was eighteen of us took a bus to Indianola, the county seat of Sunflower County, to register to vote and become first-class citizens. They only allowed me and Ernest Davis in the clerk's office.

They had a literacy test just for the Negroes. We had to say where
we lived and worked, and we were asked questions about the state
constitution dealing with "de facto" laws. I knowed as much about "de
facto" law as a horse knows about Christmas Day, so I failed but told
the clerk I would be back. When I returned to the plantation where
Pap and I lived with our two adopted daughters, I was fired from my
job and we were thrown off the plantation. Pap stood up for me and
right beside me. One time sixteen bullets were shot in the home of
a friend I stayed with when we had nowhere to go. And for a while
the only income we had was the ten dollars a week I got as a SNCC
community organizer.

In June 1963, a group of us went to a voter registration workshop in
South Carolina. We took the Trailways bus. Even though the Supreme
Court had ruled that segregated rest stops and lunch counters were
illegal, didn't make no difference, we weren't served. A highway
patrolman told us to get out, and when Annell Ponder started writing
down the license plate numbers of the police cars, she was arrested
and so was I.

In my cell, they forced me to lie face down on a bunk and ordered
two men who was prisoners there to beat me with a blackjack. I was
beat by the first Negro till he was exhausted. Then the state highway
patrolman ordered the second Negro to take the blackjack. I began to
scream, and one White man got up and began to beat me in my head
and tell me to hush. I was beat nearly to death. It was three days before
members of SNCC were allowed to take me to the hospital. After that
beating I had permanent kidney damage, a blood clot in the artery of
my left eye, and from then on, I walked with a limp.

A year later, I told that story as my testimony before the Democratic
National Committee's credentials committee, arguing on behalf of

the Mississippi Freedom Democratic Party. We wanted the MFDP
to be seated at the convention because, unlike the regular Mississippi
delegation, we weren't segregated. All of America knew about that
beating when my face and my story was on the evening news. But I
wasn't the only one got beat in the cell that day. I think about how
them Negro men were forced to beat me. I got beat, but they might
have been destroyed.

I was always working, not just to get and secure the vote, but to get
food and jobs to people in the Mississippi Delta, because it's all tied up
together, the political and social welfare. Why would a hungry man
think voting will change things? I started food co-ops and helped get
Head Start programs in Mississippi. I even ran for Congress. Didn't
win, but I knew I had the right to run.

I was always working to raise the spirits of the Movement's foot
soldiers in our meetings with songs and hymns. All that singing and
clapping of hands, and joining hands, was like a vitamin shot, boosted
our strength and helped us stay focused. My favorite song was "This
Little Light of Mine." I died of cancer and heart disease. Some people
say I couldn't have done more than I did, no matter what my history or
story had been. I died at fifty-nine years old. Hell, truth be told, I was
just getting started.

Patrisse

*Artist, organizer, educator, and popular public speaker, Patrisse Cullors
is a Los Angeles native and cofounder of the Black Lives Matter Global
Network. In 2013, Patrisse cofounded the global movement with the
viral Twitter hashtag #BlackLivesMatter which has since grown to an*

international organization with dozens of chapters around the world fighting anti-Black racism.

"When I first started organizing, I was living in a community riddled with police violence, and I still do. I was, and still am, impacted by the constant criminalization of folks in my community, including my brother and other family members. So this work isn't separate from my personal, daily life…when tragedy hits, it hits your whole self. And when burnout weighs you down, it's like an anchor on your whole being.

"I don't think I've ever learned a way to do the work without it leading to burnout. That's in part because the myth of the tireless activist is so pervasive and so effective. As organizers, we are trained that there's so much work to do and that we're the only ones able to do it. We must put our physical bodies on the line and risk our mental health and emotional health—all for the greater cause. Exhaustion is not an option.

Eventually, that becomes a really tired and problematic and painful way to live. So I am consistently trying to unlearn that. But it's hard to unlearn a thing when you're still in it. It's hard to convince yourself that it's okay to walk away from the work sometimes, in order to self-preserve. It's hard, but it is necessary."

The Story of My Body

One

I weighed three pounds, twelve ounces at birth. I fit snugly in the palms
of my mother's hands. I was so small the nurses, in astonishment,
paraded me around the halls of the maternity ward at DC's Columbia
Hospital for Women. That is the first story my mother told me about
my arrival in the world. Because I was premature, I lived the first
month of my life in an incubator. I was lucky because in the 1950s,
over ten thousand babies were blinded by excess oxygen in incubators.

Two

My mother was a forty-two-year-old woman, who, deeply dissatisfied
in her marriage, began a relationship with my father. Despite the
circumstances of my conception and birth, I was a wanted child. I
was a college sophomore when I confessed to my mother that once,
when my period had been two months late, I had considered the
possibility of having an abortion if I was pregnant. "I never once
thought of aborting you," she declared. "I thought I would be denying
the world someone special if I did that." I wasn't an inconvenience, or
an embarrassment. Maybe I was a love child. A second-chance child.
My mother had staked all she had on my father. She bet high. She
considered me the prize.

Three

I was a fast runner. On sultry summer evenings, my legs regularly carried me to victory in the races to be the first to reach the end of the block. It was a long stretch from 14th to 15th Street, past the rows of three-story Victorian houses on Harvard Street. But I mastered it. The girl racing the boys. Take a deep breath, expel it, use your arms to propel your whole self. Focus on the end of the block. Getting closer and closer. Don't look at the runners beside you. Not even for a second. And never look back.

Four

Those same legs never carried me fast enough past the men gathered in front of the neighborhood corner store. Men holding down that corner like lands they had conquered and now subjected to a tight-fisted rule. Young men. Old men. I often wondered why the corner seemed to be their home. Take a sip from the bottle of Boone's Farm in the brown bag, then strip-search the passing girls and women with a gaze. I had to abdicate possession of my body, and even my thoughts, when I walked by. I became an object for consumption.

"Smile, sister, what's wrong with you?"

Maybe I was thinking my own thoughts, my private thoughts, not knowing that I had to present a happy face to men whose happiness was fleeting or nonexistent.

"Man, look at that ass."

Now I knew how it felt to be both invisible and hyper-visible. No one ever touched me with their hands. I was squirming through the sweaty grip of words, sounds made, and language hinting at and unveiling codes of sexual conquest, possession, and need. I was twelve years old.

Five

My mother told me competing dual stories about my future. When I was ten, one day she saw me speeding past our house, in another race to be the first to reach the end of the block, and she called out to me with these words: "Come on in this house, get out of the sun. You'll have to get a light-skinned husband as it is for the sake of your children." A few years later, she told me, "One day you're going to write a book." When I was fifty-five, I sat down to write a book that finally allowed me to heal the colorist wound my mother inflicted. A wound reinforced by everything I saw and heard around me. That book helped me understand my mother and forgive her. Even more than the years of self-doubt I endured about my skin color and body image, now I mostly remember that my mother armed me with belief in the tool of writing and my proficiency in it. That belief was what I used to dismantle the hold of the ideology she'd been bequeathed and that she bequeathed to me.

Six

At nineteen, the Afro freed me to love my hair. And my face.

Seven

After graduating from college in 1972, I believed I had a body created solely by that moment in history. The pill had made pregnancy an option, not a fate. I could legally get an abortion. Orgasm, vagina, masturbation, were words we reveled in saying out loud. Words our mothers only whispered. And my young, gifted, and Black woman's body confidently strode though doors civil rights activists had broken down to claim what my parents always told me belonged to me.

As I write this I tingle with the memory of the electric energy and the strength of my twenty-two-year-old body. I didn't want a seat at the table. I wanted to call the whole room mine.

Eight

Raised in the shadow of an older sister who I thought was loved more than me and who was certain that I was loved more than her, I only wanted one child. There would be no one for that child to compete with for my love and approval. I had my one child. Akintunde Babatope Michael Kayode.

Nine

My first husband never once struck me. He never hit me with his hands. If angered, he lowered a wall of silence between us and let that emptiness do the work. Nevertheless, I felt beaten, kicked, and bruised, certain that I saw the scars on my flesh. And when he decided I'd been punished enough, he spoke. In a language that was dead to me.

Ten

In the 1950s, in my mother's boarding houses, among the people who
rented the rooms, sometimes living with us for years, husbands beat
their wives. Boyfriends beat their girlfriends. Sometimes the police
were called, but the "men in blue" usually decided, "this is a family
matter," or interrogated the woman, asking, "What did you do to make
him hit you?" I had heard women ask the same question. I saw my
parents push and shove each other in anger, pushing and shoving as
though trying to pound something into or out of their union.

Eleven

In a blind rage, when a lover told me he had slept with another woman,
I struck him. And found myself like my mother, pushing and shoving,
trying to escape, trying to find a way back to his unfaithful love.

Twelve

I looked at my body and really saw it, for the first time, when I was
fifty years old. Naked before the bathroom mirror, my eyes were
clinical. Not judgmental of the hips I had always deemed too large, the
legs I decided were too skinny, the scars from falls, the bruises from
carelessness. The flat, bunioned feet. I saw what I was made of. The
magnificent machine, spirit, body and soul. And I loved it. I thought
of the miles walked and run on those legs and feet. The incalculable
number of breaths expelled from my lungs. The tears my eyes had
shed. The laughter my throat had released. The love and fear and pain
my heart had known. The thoughts my brain gave life to. The words

my fingers and hands had written. I thought how I had always had a
home. In this body.

Becoming a New Age Strong Black Woman Means...

Celebrating yourself just because. Because you are you.
Because you deserve it. Because you don't want to reserve
celebration only for the party or the dance floor. You want
celebration of yourself to be a skill you have mastered. A skill
you employ without the need for explanation or excuse. I'm
taking a "me day" because, in the tradition of Zora Neale
Hurston, "I love myself when I'm laughing." I'm celebrating
myself by daring to claim a desire, a dream, and working
hard and smart for it to come true. I'm looking at myself in
the mirror and seeing my soul instead of a body I've been
conditioned to criticize, cause my soul is what I'm made of. I'm
training myself to celebrate myself no matter what. If I made
an error, I celebrate learning something new. If I achieved
something big, I celebrate making a way for others. I smile and
I celebrate myself.

Me Too

Studies reveal that 40–60 percent of African American girls are sexually assaulted before the age of eighteen.

I have never been raped or sexually assaulted. But as a girl, as a woman, I have been surrounded by the possibility of it all my life. During a Thanksgiving dinner one year, when I was eight or nine, a distant family member, a man with a large horse-like head, a poised yet leering smile, drew me closer to him as he sat on the stool before our upright piano in the den. The rest of the family, my parents, cousins, aunts, uncles, sat around the dinner table, amidst laughter, jokes, stories, as they recovered from the multi-course holiday meal. I don't remember how I came to be alone with this family member, a distant relation who attended family gatherings only rarely. I was a curious child and often found myself in places where I should not have been. But why shouldn't an eight- or nine-year-old girl stand in a separate orbit, a segregated space, with a male distant family member? I wore a frilly dress that day, and the crinoline slip beneath it made the skirt flower around me. As he pulled me closer, his hand rubbed my thigh. The shock of that touch sent me scurrying to my mother, who sat at the corner of the dinner table. I sidled up beside her and whispered in her ear that I had been touched. I told her who had done it.

With the skill of a diplomat, my mother turned her attention back to the table, where a story told by one of my uncles was winding down. She laughed heartily, and then rose from her seat and told me to sit down in her place. She slowly walked into the den, where the family member who touched me sat on the piano stool. I could see a mixture of guilt and fear map his face as my mother, formidable no matter her mood, approached him. She said something to him that no one could hear and he rose, walked to the sofa where piles of winter coats lay, found his jacket and his hat, and walked to the front door and left the house.

As I prepared for bed that night, my mother told me that I had done the right thing and that I was to tell her or my father any time anyone tried to touch me like that. I felt safe. Protected. By my parents. But I knew even then that there was something about my body that consigned me, because I was a girl, to the danger zone.

One of my girlfriends was raped on a date by a graduate student at the college she attended. Another was raped at a party. As is common in most cases of rape, neither woman pressed charges. They felt too much shame. They doubted their rapist would be convicted. They didn't want to relive or even remember the violation. One friend was impregnated by her rapist, had an abortion, and moved on with her life. I was the first person she told of the rape, calling me at two a.m. after crawling into bed, and in a voice that was tinier that I had ever heard it before, she told me what had happened. We must have talked for an hour. I remember apologizing over and over, as if I were the perpetrator, telling her, "I'm so sorry, so sorry." Yet, after she had the abortion, we never spoke of it again. Ever. Years later, even when she sought out the guidance of a therapist, she told me she never once mentioned the rape. "I got over it in my own way," she explained. I wondered if she really had.

Years later, I watched a professional colleague abuse alcohol, drugs, engage in increasingly unsatisfying relationships with men who were either emotionally unavailable or abusive or both. This was in the aftermath of a rape. Rape victims describe their assailants as robbers or thieves who literally stole their souls, who took something priceless and nearly irreplaceable from them. They have been robbed of peace of mind, and the ability to trust themselves or others. In return for the ransacking of their bodies and spirits, they are now owned by trauma and guilt imposed by cultural beliefs that shame victims of rape perhaps even more than those who commit the act. *"You shouldn't have gone to his apartment." "You should have dressed differently." "You shouldn't have been out that late." "You shouldn't have had anything to drink."* These are the spoken and unspoken responses often offered a rape victim, rather than an open mind and a sympathetic ear.

In every memoir class I have taught, no matter the racial make-up, writers have bravely written accounts of their rape and sexual violation. In one workshop, a fifty-year-old African American woman was writing a memoir about her journey from sexual exploitation to healing. For several years, as a child, she and her brother were sexually assaulted by a male cousin who acted as a part-time babysitter. She was also sexually violated by a female neighbor and by a male family friend. As shocking as her story was, when I asked the nine women in the class who else had been sexually assaulted, four other women raised their hands.

Given the impact of historical trauma, racism, and oppression on Black women, men, children, and Black families, in our communities, rape and sexual assault have unique dimensions. Rape and sexual assault are crimes of violence. But violence comes in many forms. There is the violence of denied opportunity. There is the violence of justice denied. There is the violence of generations-long resistance to dismantling systemic racism. Communities that have suffered consistent violations of their human rights inevitably experience higher rates of violence against women, as the men in those communities displace their anger and frustration onto the bodies of the women who are co-citizens of the same deranged reality. Women charged with working outside the home as well as caring for their families and communities often hold their anger inside, where it incubates and takes the form, sometimes, of violence, but more often of illness.

The silence, the shame, the fear of not being believed, that women across cultures feel in the wake of the act of rape, is compounded for women who have seen their communities overpoliced. If the perpetrator is a family member or member of the community, family or racial loyalty may trump the desire for justice and punishment. Families already weakened by racist policies could, in the minds of some victims, be further damaged by bringing to bear on their lives a criminal justice system that is inherently biased against them.

As a freelance writer in 1973, I wrote a major feature story on rape for *Essence* magazine. I was excited about the assignment, as I was writing it against the backdrop of an increasingly influential feminist movement that had begun publicizing lax and ineffective rape laws that discouraged women from seeking prosecution. I was excited, but also unsure if I would be able to find enough rape victims willing to be interviewed. However, once I shared my desire to speak with rape victims among friends and colleagues, over two dozen Black women contacted me. They were willing, and eager, to break their silence.

My editor wanted me to produce a story that examined not only the experience of rape victims, but also the deeper causes of the act, and delve into the lives and minds of rapists. At that time, an experimental program in a prison in New Jersey engaged men serving time for rape with group and individual therapists to uncover the unhealed traumas that led them to act out violently and to commit acts of sexual violation.

I interviewed six Black men in the program who were at various stages of clinical psychological treatment. Because they had all undergone some experience with therapy, they were able to discuss their lives, their motivations, their crimes, with enormous insight. Each man shared with me stories of childhood abuse and trauma that had gone untreated until they found themselves part of this program. As children, they had been locked in closets, sodomized, beaten violently and repeatedly, by parents or others whose actions went unreported, undiscovered, unpunished. They grew into men hoarding and crippled by a rage and anger that was as explosive and as violent as everything they had endured. They joined the military, held down jobs, married, had children, and rarely told anyone, not friends, not lovers, not wives, not family, of their abuse.

But the urge to strike out at women as vulnerable as they had once been often overtook them, transforming them into monsters even in their own eyes. One man described walking down a street one night and, at the sight of a woman across the street, suffering what can only be called a flashback to the pain he had felt during his own violation. Almost trancelike, he crossed the street, began following the woman, grabbed her, and pushed her into a deserted alley, where he raped her. The psychiatrist in charge of the treatment program told me that these men suffered from untreated trauma and stress disorder that only grew deeper and more dangerous as the years passed, as they lived seemingly normal lives. The men deserved punishment, he told me, but they also deserved treatment that would make it less likely that they would rape again.

We are, haltingly, as a culture, forming the alphabet, the syntax, the grammar of how to humanely discuss sexual violence, consent, and the meanings of yes and no. We can all become victims no matter the type of relationship we are in, same-gender, same-sex, if we self-identify as male, female, cisgender, transgender, or any other gender definition.

Tarana Burke, an African American activist who worked to support young women who were survivors of sexual abuse, first used the term "Me Too" on the pre-Facebook social platform Myspace as a way to raise awareness of sexual assault and to connect sexual assault survivors to appropriate resources. Burke was raped both as a child and as a teenager. Her mother supported her recovery and encouraged her community activism. She would create the nonprofits Just Be and Girls for Gender Equality. She has said that, when she met a young girl named Heaven in Alabama, who told her about being sexually abused by her mother's boyfriend, she didn't know what to say and never saw the girl again. She says she wishes she had said, "me too."

The phrase "Me Too" went viral as a hashtag in the midst of increasing sexual abuse allegations against film producer Harvey Weinstein. Actress Alyssa Milano encouraged women to say "Me Too" if they had experienced sexual harassment or assault. After being informed of Burke's earlier use of the term, Milano reached out to Tarana Burke, and the two women have worked together to highlight sexual violence against women.

Yet the #MeToo movement inadvertently confirmed notions about who gets heard and who gets believed. The women who came forward to first allege sexual abuse and rape by Weinstein and then testify against him in court were, in the eyes of the casual observer, privileged, rich, famous, beautiful White women. Many Black women watched the Weinstein saga unfold and wondered if #MeToo spoke to their experience. Yet the investigative journalism in the *New Yorker* and the *New York Times* that broke open the case against Weinstein revealed that these privileged, rich, famous, beautiful White women had lost careers, had feared for their lives, had thought of taking their lives, suffered post-traumatic stress, and for years were terrified of breaking their silence against a powerful man.

No conversation in the Black community about rape can be free of the stain of the historical use of the charge of rape of a White woman against a Black man by Whites as an excuse to lynch Black men. Black men have been killed for the crime of "eyeball rape," what was once called "reckless eyeballing," for merely looking at a White woman in the South. Fourteen-year-old Emmett Till was accused of making a pass at the wife of a White store owner in Money, Mississippi, in 1955, and lynched. His killers went unpunished. In 1973, Till's accuser admitted her claim against Till was a lie. The Black man as an oversexed, out-of-control sexual predator seeking to prey on innocent White women became a powerful trope during and after slavery. Its echoes persist today.

We have been rebuked and scorned and subject to conspiracies of all kinds designed to cripple our progress and "bring down" our leaders. And any Black man or woman who gains political or cultural prominence, by default, becomes a race leader, a "credit to the race."

As a result of a tangled, twisted history in which Black men have been routinely and often unfairly demonized, we extend immunity to powerful Black men who are the subject of allegations of crimes, and especially crimes against women. If the singer R. Kelly had been raping underage White teenaged girls and imprisoning them in his home, it would have not taken twenty years to arrest him. Kelly benefitted from his ability, as a wealthy music mega-star, to pressure and threaten journalists, juries that refused to convict him, legions of mostly Black female fans who refused to believe the charges or saw them as another attempt to destroy a Black man, and the cultural devaluation of Black female experience and pain, even by some Black women.

A powerful documentary, *Surviving R. Kelly*, released during the highly publicized revelations of abuse of a group of White women, created the environment in which Kelly's crimes against Black women could finally gain long-overdue national attention, meaningful legal action, and the singer's long-delayed reckoning. Because so many of the women accusing Bill Cosby of sexual abuse were White, many in the Black community disregarded their allegations out of hand. Yet the legitimate fear that the downfall of a prominent Black man has been "engineered" has to be chastened with logic, objectivity, and the patterns of the alleged behavior as well as extending compassion to those making the charge. Just as Southern Whites once always judged Black men inherently guilty of a rape charge, too many Black men and women reflexively deem charges of sexual misconduct against prominent Black men false. We have to begin to determine what is in our own individual best interest. We have the right to assert the primacy of own interests, health, and well-being within a culture and within families that too often call for self-sacrifice and silence—that require us to be Strong Black Women. Drew Dixon, a prominent and influential former music producer, who along with nine other women has charged music mogul Russell Simmons with rape, said of her decision not to report the abuse and the decade-long journey to finally going public with the charge, "As a Black woman I didn't know if the #MeToo movement applied to me. I didn't want to add fire to the myth of the dangerous Black male sexual predator. I took one for the team. I didn't want to let the culture down."

Drew Dixon's story was told in a moving documentary, *On the Record*. After leaving Def Jam records and trying to recover emotionally from the alleged sexual assault by Simmons, Dixon moved to Arista Records, where her career was again derailed, she says, when she refused the sexual advances of CEO L. A. Reid, who has denied the charge. Dixon was a brilliant, groundbreaking producer who was an early producer of hip hop and who worked with Aretha Franklin, Lauryn Hill, Notorious B.I.G., and Mary J. Blige, among others. To speak about sexual harassment and abuse, she correctly assumed, would mean losing the career she loved, being subjected to a smear campaign, and possibly being unsupported by friends and family. In the film, we meet several other Black women who say they were victimized sexually by Simmons.

It was impossible not to notice that these were light-skinned Black women, women who, in the eyes of the Black community, represented the ideal of beauty because of their skin color and features. Women who both are sought-after, and can often be victimized savagely, because of their assumed "superiority." High-profile Black men want these women as trophy and conquest. For my book *Don't Play in the Sun: One Woman's Journey Through the Color Complex*, I interviewed a prominent Black female therapist who described the toxic emotions that light-skinned women can inspire in some Black men. "They love them because they are light and hate them for the same reason," she said. "And for some men, the act of rape is a way of pushing those women off the pedestal our community has placed them on. A pedestal that hypersexualizes and robs light-skinned women of individuality, personhood, and as recipients of compassion." In 2017, L. A. Reid was forced to step down as chairman of Epic Records after multiple allegations of sexual misconduct.

Drew Dixon saw media representations of the #MeToo movement that presented White female victims of rape and sexual assault publicly supporting other White female victims. Absent were images of #MeToo as a statement for all women, no matter their race, ethnicity, class, or gender identity. So doubts about the relevance of the movement to her situation were reasonable. When I watched the documentary, her admission that she "didn't want to let the culture down" haunted me, and still breaks my heart. "The culture." A culture within which Black women must be strong enough to bear abuse in silence—a silence that is defined as strength. A culture of disbelief. A culture of holding victims to a higher standard of proof than those who victimize them. A culture that protects the rich and powerful from censure or legal action. A culture of silence. A culture that makes racial loyalty the litmus tests the aggrieved must pass. A culture desperately in need of reimagination.

Becoming A New Age Strong Black Woman Means...

> **Talking about our bodies**. Talking to our daughters about sexual consent, but also about sexual gratification. What their bodies can feel, the difference between pain and pleasure, and how they are masters of their bodies. Talking about how to protect themselves from sexually transmitted diseases, and emotional manipulation in their relationships.

Fear Loathing Love: Our Bodies Inside Out

The Things We Carry

Deconstructing the stereotypes, mythology, and misinformation that too often define our health and ill-health is a necessary prelude to any meaningful discussion about our bodies. Let's start by talking about fat. In the Black community, we have long seen big women as voluptuous, beautiful, sexy, powerful. Some of our most talented, valued, and impactful cultural icons and artists have been big women. Ethel Waters, Ma Rainey, Big Mama Thornton. And the singer Lizzo is loved as much for the way she has turned love of her big body into a near-religion as for her joyous performance and soulful singing. White women, White society, are finally *catching up to us* in their current acknowledgement that a big body can be beautiful, strong, and healthy.

Our acceptance of the big female body exists beside that fact that for decades, studies of obesity have determined that African American women are consistently more obese than White women. The body mass index (BMI) is the formula for this conclusion. What is BMI? It is a person's weight in kilograms divided by the square of their height in meters. BMI can be used to screen for weight categories that may lead to health problems. We often think of BMI when considering obesity, but it identifies underweight as well. The BMI has long been considered the unquestioned determination of obesity. Increasingly it has been denounced as "bogus," irrelevant, and even dangerous, for a variety of reasons, ranging from the fact that it was originally designed to measure the body mass of populations, not individuals, and the illogic of its one-size-fits-all reasoning.

What is obesity? Obesity is defined as excess weight that poses a danger to health because it puts you at risk for Type 2 diabetes, high cholesterol, stroke, and heart disease. And with or without the BMI test, we know that Black women are disproportionately obese and overweight.

This is the muddled backdrop against which many of us are chiseling away at the hardened core of the legacy of annihilation of Black women's confidence in and love of their bodies. There is a medical industry using a tool that is inadequate and possibly misleading. There are the competing images we possess of large Black bodies despised by the dominant society, yet accepted and even praised within our community. There is the undeniable knowledge that obesity and being overweight are health risks. We are erased and excluded from important medical studies and clinical trials. For many of us, a visit to the doctor's office means having our complaints about pain ignored because of the still-prevalent racist belief that our threshold for pain is higher than that of Whites. If the requests by Serena Williams and Beyoncé for specific treatments and medication during and after their experiences giving birth were met with skepticism and resistance by health professionals, many Black women may wonder, how could *they* leave the doctor's office with their lives?

And yet, half of all Black girls will develop diabetes. Eighty percent of Black women are overweight or obese, and Black women die of preventable obesity-related illnesses (stroke and heart attack) *more than anyone else* in America. Illnesses that could be prevented or managed with changes in diet and levels of activity.

Black women's lower resting metabolism and higher rate of insulin resistance accounts for our "thickness," our curves, and overall body size. And studies show that we can be big and be healthy. Still, we are near collapse from the weight of the innumerable micro and macro risk factors inherent in our daily lives. An overweight White woman does not have her excess weight supercharged, made more deadly by the interaction of that weight with the impact of systemic racism on her body.

My grandmother and my mother were overweight. They both died of obesity-related diseases. Obesity was a major factor in my mother's early death. Obesity gave her high blood pressure and an unhealthy heart. Her right and ability to live her life, to try to fulfill her dreams, love and support me, was cut short by obesity. Even if you are not obese, if you are overweight, you are more likely to develop health challenges.

Writer Alice Randall wrote about her struggle to attain and maintain a healthy weight and observed, "Many Black women are fat because we want to be. How many White girls in the '60s grew up praying for fat thighs? I know I did. I asked God to give me big thighs like my dancing teacher, Diane. There was no way I wanted to look like Twiggy, the White model whose boy-like build was the dream of White girls. Not with Joe Tex ringing in my ears. How many middle-aged White women fear their husbands will find them less attractive if their weight drops to less than 200 pounds? I have yet to meet one. But I know many Black women whose sane, handsome, successful husbands worry when their women start losing weight. My lawyer husband is one." As I read Randall's essay, I remembered that even *my* husband, watching me perform yoga or Pilates, occasionally urges me "not to lose too much weight."

We need a radically new and revised consciousness about our bodies.
A consciousness that allows us to talk without shame or judgment
about how excess weight is killing us. What are the things we carry?
And how much do they weigh?

Dr. Joy DeGruy, author of *Post Traumatic Slave Syndrome: America's
Legacy of Enduring Injury and Healing*, describes post-traumatic
slave syndrome as "a condition that exists when a population has
experienced multigenerational trauma resulting from centuries of
slavery and continues to experience oppression and institutionalized
racism today." African Americans carry the mark, the stain, *the weight*,
of PTSS. The lies and silence and hypocrisy that render impossible
the kind of scorching, cleansing, and redemptive discussion about
the impact of slavery and racism in America that we need as a nation
has infected Whites with the intergenerational disease of racism
and Blacks with a mutilated sense of self and of our bodies that is
devouring us.

Our bodies are a testament to all that we as a nation within a nation
have endured. Intergenerational racial and other traumas create
stress that negatively alters brain capacity, growth, and function, and
increases the likelihood of obesity. When we look at the bodies of
so many overweight and obese Black women, we are seeing untold
stories, stories of abuse, and muffled pain. Clinical social worker and
social psychologist Dr. Pamela Brewer has concluded that "Black
women are too often gorging on toxic emotions in an effort to find
emotional safety. Many Black women feel that if they are larger, they

are more solid, they literally have substance and power, especially if they have suffered trauma."

When I talk about obesity, I am talking about health. Health, not beauty, health, not intrinsic value, health, not the significance of an individual's life. Obesity is dangerous because it shortens our life possibilities, and life span. Our inability to talk honestly about this topic is a reflection of the national silence about obesity as a killer of more and more Americans of all races and ages. We can talk about obesity and contextualize the discussion by recognizing the issues of economics, lack of access to good health care, class, education, employment, that make it more difficult for Black women to actively engage in the kind of self-care that defeats obesity. But we are in crisis and we have to acknowledge that.

The Strong Black Woman syndrome, a response to racism that conditions Black women to believe they must excel and overachieve on the job, at home, and in all situations, to prove their value to themselves and others, and that the needs of others come first, exacts a high price—the minimizing of the need for self-care. Self-care that could minimize overweight and obesity.

The highly educated, professional, well-paid "white-collar sister" working in a corporate setting is likely enduring as much stress as a "blue-collar sister" working a minimum-wage job. In both cases, the women may find that their ambition and desire to rise in the workplace is met with resentment, pushback, as well as racist and sexist responses. They may be overlooked for promotion despite working "twice as hard." Both women are likely "anchors" in their families, emotionally and financially, and have no meaningful outlet for the stress they feel. Because of pay disparities based on gender and race, both women may find themselves working "overtime" in order to make up the difference.

The demands of work and family may convince both women that they have little time to think about eating healthy time to prepare healthy meals or even eat them, so they eat on the run, and several days a week eat "fast food." Let's get personal in this hypothetical and give these sisters names. Sabrina, the "white-collar sister" has an excellent health care plan thanks to her high paying job, but she is thirty-five and thinks that annual checkups are only for old people, so she hasn't been to see her doctor in two years. Eden, the "blue-collar sister" doesn't have health coverage on her job and uses the emergency room for herself and her son when they get sick.

Sabrina doesn't go to the gym in her building even though her job pays for it. It seems like too much trouble, she worries about sweating out her hair, and her lunch break is the one time during the workday when she can escape the stress of her office. And after work, she has to hurry home to relieve her sister who is caring for their elderly mother. Eden doesn't have a gym in her neighborhood, doesn't have a car, and is so exhausted from standing on her feet all day on her job, picking her son up from day care, and shopping, that exercise is the last thing on her mind. Sabrina is obese and Eden is overweight. Neither one of them knows that their excess weight could lead to a stroke or a heart attack. Both suffer from undiagnosed depression. Neither woman is aware of her family's medical history and how that affects them.

Sometimes, when they are very brave, they allow themselves for a moment to think about their weight, but thinking about it only makes them feel bad, and they don't know where or how to start to talk about being healthy, although healthy is what they really want to be.

Both Sabrina and Eden fear that recognition of a health issue will sabotage their self-image as Strong Black Women—women who live in a world that marginalizes or ignores them as they struggle to present themselves as capable, in charge, and in control. Sabrina knows she is obese, but is terrified to have a doctor confirm her fears. She doesn't just want to lose weight. She wants to shed her belief that her body is unlovable, and that, if her body is unlovable, then so is she. Who will hold her hand as she walks this road? She isn't used to asking for help. She is a Strong Black Woman.

We can create a new scenario if we talk about health, talk about overweight and obesity as a health issue, and create the spaces, the institutional and community support, to enable Black women to pursue and maintain health.

Black women have a long and proud tradition of fearless leadership. We have to lead in this effort too. For ourselves, for our families, for our communities. Our health is personal and political. We have to actively engage in self-care and push through our votes and activism for universal, easily affordable, easily accessed health care for all. That means pressing those who represent us to make healthcare for all a reality.

Even as we acknowledge how racism has impacted the ways in which we think about being overweight or obese, it is crucial to *actually see* Black women and not just our size. Even as America "normalizes" obesity and simultaneously lionizes the thin, and the "fit," the excess weight "big girls" carry renders them invisible, and they struggle to be seen and acknowledged, known and loved. We are not just victims of racism. We are women, sisters, friends, mothers, lovers, workers, artists, inventors, leaders. But sometimes our bodies are a potential death sentence, and we have to face that and then fight it.

Because I saw what being overweight did to my mother's health, I swore that I would fight to be healthy. And yet my mother's body was the site not only of literal weight, but also of grief, grieving, and memories. Memories of three "failed" marriages and the loss of her financial autonomy and power when, in the aftermath of leaving my father, she lost several boarding houses that she had owned. Memories of money that my father squandered. Memories of love and devotion to men who left her bereft and vanquished. A loss of a sense of purpose as she grew older. Fear that she would die before I completed high school, and then college. Regret. Guilt.

These are the things that *I know* she carried—the excess baggage of her life, accumulated at a steady pace, that she could find no way to unload. There is no way that I can, or am brave enough to, imagine the things she carried that *I don't know*. My genes were encoded with the drama of my mother's unsatisfying relationships with men, and I mimicked her habits. And yet with all she carried, and perhaps because of all she carried, she made me who I became. She was more than the weight of her burdens. My mother was the promise of a huge giving heart, the love she had for her family, her compassion for others, and the affection she gave to and received from her life-giving circle of friends.

My sister was dying. My husband and I sat at her bedside in a rehabilitation center where she had been living for nearly a year. Her hands were gnarled and useless as a result of rheumatoid arthritis, and she could no longer walk and had to use a wheelchair. Joe and I sat at her bedside on a fall Sunday afternoon six months before her death. She was seventy-eight years old. Her death would be the result of vascular dementia, often caused by a stroke or other type of damage to the blood vessels, impacting their ability to deliver blood to the brain and causing a reduction in proper brain function. These visits had become a gift to me. I hoped they were a gift to her. The only thing that mattered when I walked into her room was that she was my sister. Past hurts, pain, had been evicted from both our hearts. When I leaned over to kiss her hello or kiss her goodbye, more than once, her eyes searching and discovering me with a kind of awe, she whispered, "Marita, you're beautiful."

We talked of the mundane and the ordinary. Joe asked her what country she would go to first when she left the rehabilitation center. Which restaurant? She laughed and played along. She wanted to go to an island in the Caribbean, and she would go to a fancy steak house. I read a paragraph from one of my books, showed her a photo of my nine-year-old step-granddaughter. We discovered the magnificence of the ordinary. It was enough to be in and sit in her presence. Why had we ever needed more than this? Now we didn't want or need anything more. Jean was my adopted sister, but we were raised by the same mother, and so we were sisters.

Jean was not obese, but my sister's body was nonetheless, swollen, bloated, misshapen by the things she carried. She was adopted by my mother and her second husband. My mother left that husband for my father. My sister carried the pain of being told by my mother and other relatives that she was not adopted when she suspected that she was. In the 1940s and '50s, it was felt that it was best to hide birth history from an adopted child. After years of questioning family members and growing increasingly frustrated by being stonewalled, through a family member who worked at DC Health's Vital Records Division, Jean was given proof that she had indeed been adopted. My mother's lie was considered, in that era, an act of love.

But I am certain that my sister was dogged by unanswered questions about her birth parents and why she was given up. She must have felt abandoned by the unknown birth family and anger at my mother for shielding her from the truth. I don't think she ever forgave my mother. Only now can I understand the years of anguish and depression Jean must have experienced. And the guilt my mother could only try vainly to hide. This was a mother-daughter crisis that was never solved.

I was born when she was ten. My father was the reason my mother left the only father my sister had known. She was broken and heartbroken and remained in some ways beyond repair.

My sister was always surrounded by people whose laughter and presence kept the demons and ghosts and questions and pain away. It was important for Jean to appear to be happy. To smile. To be a Strong Black Woman. What was the cost of all that pretense? Over the years, she tried to beat back and through the anger and pain and questions that ravaged her body. For a lot of her life, my sister was unwell. How much did that weigh?

Jean was a small woman who raised five boys into men, mostly on her own, but with the help of various and varying extended families, where she found the love I think she felt she was denied in our home by our mother. This tiny woman, who was smart and funny and sharp and worked an administrative-level job in the hotel industry, now lay in a small bed swathed in sheets and blankets, and here at last we had found each other. My sister was a Strong Black Woman. She buckled, but kept bearing the weight. I am sure that all she ever wanted to know is what we all yearn to know: who am I? Five years before the day Joe and I sat at her bedside, my sister had lost three of her sons in a year and a half, one to suicide. How had my sister borne such loss? How has she risen to meet each new day?

Like every family, mine was entangled in a feverish and fevered tango with secrets, lies, and truth. A dance that was more burden than release. The weight my sister carried was borne by us all, packed in boxes of varying sizes. We all groaned, trying to navigate the path of our lives while carrying all that was spoken and all that was unsaid.

I was asked to write and read the words that she could not speak at the funerals for two of her sons, my nephews. Sorrow had made her mute. I was the family writer, and so… And yet, as I sat beside her bed that day, my sister was light, nearly weightless. So was I. Twice, she had been near death, but my sister was strong. She had a will of steel. She would go when she was ready. Everything we had ever needed to say we spoke in those final visits. The articulation of the message was in the calm acceptance of our forever sisterhood which had no expiration date. We weren't heavy. We were sisters.

Black women are learning how to tell a new story about their bodies. We do not possess a death wish. We want to live. Trapped in a whirlwind, outnumbered by forces often beyond our control, we are dancing as fast as we can. The nonprofit organization Girl Trek has sparked a nationwide health revolution as its nearly one million Black female members commit to a regimen of walking for health and fitness. For over almost forty years, the Black Women's Health Initiative has surveyed Black women all over America about their health, and lobbies for policy changes to meet our health challenges. Black women of all ages are creating and finding community on social media to address their health challenges. Along with the NAACP and the Urban League, Black women, the bedrock of Black churches, are creating church-based programs to promote health. Sororities and other Black women's groups are supporting annual initiatives that encourage discussion of health. We can do this.

Who Is the Fairest of Them All?

In her book *Ain't I A Beauty Queen?: Black Women, Beauty, and the Politics of Race,* Maxine Leeds Craig traces the long historical trend of offering multiracial women up as the "ideal type" of Black woman. In the early nineteen hundreds, according to one of the preeminent Black newspapers of the late nineteenth and twentieth centuries, the *New York Age,* this woman was defined as having "A well balanced and symmetrical head, full slender neck, the features clear cut, with the appearance of being chiseled rather than cast;…a fine Negro nose with a trace of the Egyptian and a slight aquiline curve; the mouth fairly small but well-proportioned and a slightly pointed, round, firm chin… the marvelously fine curving eyelash of which the Negro race can be justly proud."

Craig notes that this "ideal" Black woman is of "mixed racial heritage" and, although hair type and skin color were not explicitly stated, the desire for long hair and light skin was "so firmly established" that it "went without saying." This is an aesthetic that is unachievable for most Black women, yet is supposed to be a symbol of her "finest expression," that of a partially White racial heritage. The opposing construction of Black skin or too-Black features, by Whites and Blacks, as "ugly" locks many Black women outside of the definition of beauty and femininity. This is the operative and accepted definition of beauty for much of the world.

Colorism is a global mental health issue negatively impacting communities of brown and Black people around the world, from Asia to Africa to America. Dark and light women are strangers to themselves and one another. Dark girls can never be pretty, smart, feminine, valuable enough. Light girls can never be Black enough, trusted enough by dark girls, their experience in all its nuance understood enough. Dark girls are desexualized, light girls are hypersexualized. Coming of age in the midst of the Black Power and Black cultural revolutions liberated me in defining ways as I grew into womanhood and Black womanhood. Today the wide-angle public mirror I look into no longer reflects back at me the oppressive monolith of absolute and unchallenged preeminence of lighter-skinned women in public spaces. In twentieth-century literature, Nella Larsen and Zora Neale Hurston dramatized, interrogated, and satirized "passing" as well as the deeply entrenched colorist beliefs accepted as gospel. In my fiction, inevitably and purposefully, I have created brown to Black female protagonists who are complex and complicated and desired.

Political, economic, and social changes, challenges, and upheavals have placed more and more Black women in positions where they can create and are creating media (visual arts, films, TV, videos, literature) that complicates our ideas about colorism. They are creating media in which brown to Black women are loved, sought-after, where they are not locked into playing Black women who are "angry" and "tough," but now can choose roles where they are vulnerable and complex. These women creatives are giving us narratives in which women who

benefit from "pretty privilege" or who are biracial and considered
exotic, whose light skin is a currency in and of itself, often speak
their truth of isolation from other Black women and their desire for
sisterhood that is colorblind. Beyoncé, Mariah Carey, Alicia Keyes, and
Rihanna reign as global symbols of acceptable "Black beauty" in the
world of music. Their "beauty" is embedded in the idea that it springs
from Whiteness, but it is the offspring of Blackness too.

How and why their color has elevated them is open for wide-ranging
discussion and critique, and the women themselves actively promote
opportunities in a rigidly sexist and colorist industry for women many
shades darker than them. *This is new. This is healing.* Black actresses
and producers and writers Ava Duvernay, Katori Hall, Viola Davis,
Lupita Nyong'o, Danai Gurira, Issa Rae, Taraji P. Henson, Octavia
Spencer, Rutina Wesley, Regina King, Lena Waithe, Michaela Coel,
and Slick Woods are creating the kind of "content" that does more
than entertain. It hypnotizes. It socializes. It inspires. It questions. It
answers. What is most exciting is that this is a woefully incomplete list
of the Black female genius finding and claiming expression. Expression
that has a global impact. As these revolutionary images stream across
international borders on our screens, women everywhere can see
themselves as never before and see other women creating realistic
images of themselves as never before. *This is new. This is healing.*
Colorism has not been unearthed, but it is now more than ever before
on the defensive. I believe in the power of Black women and their allies
to keep coloring outside the lines of outdated and irrelevant definitions
of beauty and worth.

Becoming A New Age Strong Black Woman Means...

Talking about our bodies The love and care and maintenance they require, and how much our bodies give us, how they keep us going, even when we neglect them.

Talking about our bodies. How they have to move in order to be healthy and that there are exercises for people of all sizes, abilities, ages, and strength levels. Are we asking more of our bodies than they can provide? We don't live in our bodies alone. Our hearts and kidneys and livers, and brains, all have a vote. They can all rebel or go on strike if trapped in an environment that is corrupting their healthy functioning.

Talking about our bodies. Annual checkups and dentist appointments and massages and walks in our neighborhood or tuning into the sisters on YouTube doing cardio. And swimming and sweating, which releases toxins and sweating some more, or joining a gym.

Talking about how, at sixty-eight, I overcame my fear of deep water by learning to swim in the deep end of the pool (thirteen feet), how to breathe correctly in the deep end and feel my body strong, purposeful, graceful, and strong. Talking about how my body hums for the rest of the day after an hour in the pool. In the deep end.

Talking about walking five miles with my eighty-one-year-old friend to raise money for Alzheimer's research.

Talking about our bodies and telling them thank you.

Falling: Days of Dying, Rage and Redemption

"People think of frontline workers, transit workers, the first responders, cops, firefighters, as having helped the city get through it. But that's not what happened. We helped the city survive it. I'm saturated with grief and anger."

—New York City bus driver Terence Layne on the experience of "pandemic trauma"

We came to think of them as twin pandemics: one a virus whose arrival was to most of us a surprise, a shock to the system, even as scientists knew its arrival was inevitable; the other, racism, a disease that had morphed into new forms and shapes even as we thought the march of history, decades of activism, new cultural changes and laws, had nearly defeated it. The World Health Organization defined coronavirus (COVID-19) as an infectious disease caused by a newly discovered coronavirus. While most people who become infected develop a mild case, those with underlying medical issues, such as diabetes, cancer, high blood pressure, or heart disease, develop a serious illness that is often fatal. Droplets of saliva in a discharge from an infected person who coughs, or sneezes, or talks loudly can spread the disease.

COVID-19 spreads more easily than the flu, causes more serious illness in some people, takes longer before people are symptomatic, and those infected with it can be contagious much longer. As the virus mutated, more of those who were young and healthy were also struck and sometimes died.

The perennial pandemic of racism has infected America since its founding, literally and figuratively sickening and shortening the lifespans of generations of Black people, yet inoculating Whites against recognition of it or a reckoning with its impact, and the negative effect of racism on Whites goes largely unexplored and unrecognized.

The initial phase of the COVID-19 pandemic forced us into lockdown, separation from one another, and a three-month quarantine. As we uneasily, hesitantly ventured out, the video that captured the death of George Floyd being choked under the knee of a White Minneapolis police officer, Derek Chauvin, drove many of us—jobless, or wounded from meager salaries and no healthcare safety net, victimized by the inept government response to the pandemic, grieving twenty thousand dead in New York City—into the streets in protest throughout the country.

A friend told me that all of this, every part of it, was ordained. The year 2020, she said, is a year of clarified and sharpened vision; 20/20 is considered "perfect vision." If infected with COVID-19, it is difficult to breathe. George Floyd died because he couldn't breathe. In the Bible 20 is a symbol of waiting. In numerology, 20 is the beginning of a new decade. Transformation. Big time. I don't have to believe or not believe in God or the Devil or angels to know that what I lived through, what filled my TV and computer screens, was in the truest sense earth-shattering, as Confederate statues were pulled from their moorings

from Mississippi to Washington, DC. Everything was falling…
into place?

Black and brown people in the US were disproportionately impacted
by COVID-19. The combination of underlying medical issues and the
invasive impact of racism on all aspects of their lives meant that the
disease discriminated against them. Three months into the pandemic
in Washington, DC, while African Americans were 44 percent of the
population, they were 74 percent of the COVID-19 deaths. One report
stated in June 2020 that, if they had died of COVID-19 at the same rate
as White Americans, at least 14,400 Black Americans, 1,200 Latino
Americans, and 200 Indigenous Americans would still be alive.

The disease impacted women overall and the types of jobs they had
with special vigor. Black women sustained disproportionate losses
of both life and livelihood. They put their lives at risk in low-wage
caretaking jobs. Jobs that often provided no benefits. Not working
put their livelihoods in limbo; working put their lives in jeopardy.
The previously invisible workers deemed "essential" during the
pandemic—postal workers, delivery people, cashiers, nurses caring for
the elderly—suddenly became glaringly visible.

Less than a month after George Floyd's death, police reform
measures—from the radical to the conservative—revelations
of systemic police racism and misconduct, all became part of a
conversation that many had long thought impossible to begin or
sustain. The CEO of Netflix and his wife donated $120 million to
HBCUs (historically Black colleges and universities); the Floyd
family's GoFundMe Page collected $13 million in donations. Books
about race and racism topped the bestseller lists; White people called
their Black friends to apologize for White racism; Aunt Jemima and
Uncle Ben were retired; schools, Hollywood, the publishing industry,

every profession responded to the demands of African Americans for redress and new policies to root out and defeat systemic racism. And Black and brown men were found publicly hanged. Near City Hall in Palmdale, California. From a tree in Victorville, California. From trees near a park and an elementary school in Texas. Black women began buying guns and learning how to shoot them. White militias swore to defend White supremacy to the death. The rates of depression and anxiety in the African American community shot up. When I emailed Dr. Kanika Bell in Atlanta, where Rayshard Brooks was shot in the back by a White police officer eighteen days after George Floyd became victim, martyr, and symbol, and asked how her clients were faring, she emailed back that many were suffering insomnia, suicidal thoughts, and increasing anxiety.

I thought again and again about "Speech Sounds," Octavia Butler's award-winning science fiction short story about a society in which, due to a global environmental catastrophe, some people have lost the ability to read and speak while others have lost the ability to write, and everyone suffers from some diminished capacity to communicate. I often teach the story as a masterpiece of structure and style, as well as for its compelling message about the chaos that results when the ability to communicate is lost or fractured. The story is a stark dramatization of how much we depend on the ability to understand one another to maintain not just law and order, but the crucial bonds of humanity that connect us one to another.

Scenes and Meditations from Quarantine

The constant replay of the video deaths of these victims of police execution feels like a form of re-enslavement, a psychological assault, an emotional rape. For CNN and MSNBC and the news outlets who charge advertisers more when viewership goes up, as it always does when the nation is gripped by politics or protests, it is a simple decision—about money. The more the videos are aired, the more people tune in to see them, which means more people are watching, so Toyota and Target and GEICO pay more to reach the increasing number of viewers with their product promotions. It is a simple decision for me too. I cannot watch them. And the not watching is not just to ensure my mental health, but becomes a form of political protest. The replay of the collapse of the Twin Towers on 9/11 had given me insomnia. The police murder videos filled me with dread, fear, and paranoia.

Black bodies and Black lives have always been a spectacle for the White gaze. When the ship the *White Lion* brought twenty captured Africans to Jamestown, Virginia, in 1619, where they were enslaved a year before the Pilgrims landed at Plymouth Rock, those men and women, survivors of a hellhole death trap stood before the first Whites who saw them as sin turned into flesh. On the auction block the sale of Black people was commerce, curiosity, festival, open to White men, women, and children. We could be and were sold everywhere, from kitchens to backyards to roadsides and dining rooms. Any place in America could become a slave pen. Lynchings had a carnival, celebratory atmosphere. And the current age of videos of Black men, Black women, Black youth being beaten and killed by police continues the spectacle. Five-minute, ten-minute clips that have become an invention as American as jazz or rock and roll.

I talked about race and racism with my son Michael from the time he was three or four. I had to. There was no one moment when we had "the talk." "The talk" is a perpetual conversation in African American homes. And whether it is the talk about how to be polite when stopped by the police, to keep your hands in view and not make any sudden moves, or how to bounce back when denied a job or promotion or loan and you know the way you know your name it was denied because of race, "the talk" always tastes like ashes in my mouth. I am always amazed that I don't choke on the words, their bitterness and betrayal, and how little comfort or explanation they offer.

My son was brutalized by a Black cop when he was seventeen because he ran a red light. My six-foot-three son was yanked out of the car, thrown first on the hood of the car and then on the ground, and handcuffed. The cop had a long list of previous complaints, and it would take a year for the review of the case to deem that he had not used excessive force, despite breaking my son's arm. When researching a novel a year later about a Black cop who kills a young man during a stop, I interviewed a dozen Black cops who confirmed that they all profiled young Black men.

After a while, I couldn't sleep. I didn't watch the videos, but my husband goes to sleep with Trevor Noah of *The Daily Show* and wakes up to have breakfast with Amy Goodman of *Democracy Now,* so the clouds of mourning filled our home. In the soundproof basement I could find some respite, but I was crying without shedding a tear, screaming without making a sound. And because I am a writer, I wanted to write something, anything to share with people. It took me weeks, but finally I found words, and words found me, and this is what I posted.

I Can't Breathe, but I Can Still Write

I used to never remember my dreams. Now I cannot forget them.

I can't breathe, but I can still write, so I will tell you about my dreams.

People all over the world felt that knee on their neck.

America is now the kind of country we would normally invade. A persecuted minority protests in the streets, sympathetic members of the majority join in, and the protests are met with overwhelming force. A crippled legislative branch, a corrupt executive, mass unemployment, policies that support the spread of the pandemic. Softened up and easy to invade because of a coronavirus pandemic preceded by a pandemic of mass shootings and a perennial pandemic of racism.

I can't breathe, but I can still write.

I salute the thousands of Whites marching in the streets of America. But America keeps finding new ways to betray my trust, so I have to ask…will the White woman holding the sign "White silence is violence" on Black Lives Matter Square near the White House *not* marginalize the token Black person in her office? Will she advocate for the promotion of a qualified Black person to be *her boss?*

Will she not call the police because there is a Black man she says she has never seen before (he lives three doors down) walking his dog on *her* street? It used to be *his* street (that's how we think in America). Will she speak truth to power when she is the only White person in the room inclined to do so? Or will she need the safety of the crowd? Will she stop reading *How to Be an Anti-Racist* and just be an antiracist?

I can't breathe, but I can still write, and I can still dream.

Can we break bread together? At her house or mine?

Yes, it's past time to retire Uncle Ben and Aunt Jemima, but the meal I really want to sit down to is an appetizer of justice, an entree of equality, and the dessert of Black wealth.

I have fingers crossed that our new White allies will roll up their sleeves and do the work.

I can't breathe, but I can still write.

Writers are disciplined dreamers. Like the people in the streets. Returning day after day because they cannot resist the monumental task of creation. Everything is a story, whether it is an anthem or a blueprint for police reform. There is the ragged, rugged first draft, all emotion and pain, graffiti turned into eloquence and art. There is the second draft, when the writer faces doubt, uncertainty that is an emotional form of tear gas, a psychological line of police. There is the continuing search as the writer opens herself up to, listens for, the meaning and the message, allows it to chart its own course, say everything, knowing everything must be said in order to dive deep and dredge up into the light the story's battered pulse. We are all writers now.

Defund…Reform…Reimagine. This is the language of crisis, of emergency. The language of hope rather than despair. The pushback will be brutal, but remember what Sam Cooke said about change.

I can't breathe, but I can still write.

The perpetrators of anti-Black violence are writers too. Bad writers. Dangerous writers. Fear and terror and hate writers. Their story is a story that extinguishes life and community and hope. A story that some find comfort in. Two competing stories. I know which one I will write. I know which one I will read.

In my living room, my son and daughter-in-law stand six feet away from my husband and me. We are all wearing masks as they tell us they are expecting a child. The baby will be a girl. Damn social distancing! I hug them both. We have to learn how to breathe again. For my granddaughter. For all the babies. *Black Lives Matter.*

P.S. Black absorbs all colors.

Black Americans continued to die disproportionately of COVID-19 because disparities were not addressed on the local, state, or federal level, even in cities run by Black mayors, like Atlanta, Baltimore, and Washington, DC, or in Prince Georges County, where I live, headed by a Black female County Executive. But there were heartening exceptions.

Garlin Gilchrist II, a Detroit native as well as Michigan's lieutenant governor, formed one of the nation's first state racial disparities task forces on COVID-19 in April 2020.

From a *Washington Post* article on the continuing racial disparities in COVID-19 deaths and care:

"Faced with extreme disparities in COVID-19 deaths, Michigan officials in April 2020 undertook a series of steps, from boosting testing to connecting people of color with primary care doctors. When state epidemiologists ran the numbers in September, they found a huge change: Black residents who in April accounted for 29.4 percent of cases and 40.7 percent of deaths now made up only 8 percent of cases and 10 percent of deaths, very similar to their percentage in the population. Gilchrist emphasized the state's efforts had not been complicated. 'I think the reason we have been able to make progress is we chose to focus on it,' he said."

By the time I finished the final draft of this book, more than 600,000 Americans had died of COVID-19, a number that is officially acknowledged as an undercount. Three and a half million people had died of COVID-19 worldwide. In the fall of 2020, a vaccine had been developed. The Pfizer/BioNTech vaccine was followed by vaccines developed by Moderna and Johnson & Johnson.

Against the backdrop of a pandemic that was deeply personal and seemed to impact every aspect of our lives, Black women were questioning the Strong Black Woman Syndrome. Social media became a virtual venue for Black women to share the pressures they felt and to question why they felt the need to do everything and be everything to everyone. Black women were struggling to find new ways to be healthy even as they felt their health was under siege. Black women who had not walked or exercised began doing both.

We Walk With Harriet is a group of eight Black women, aged thirty-eight to sixty-five, who trained for months to retrace Harriet Tubman's 116-mile Underground Railroad trek from Cambridge, Maryland, to Kennett Square, Pennsylvania. When Linda Harris, sixty-five, of Mitchellville, Maryland, re-read *Runaway Slave: The Story of Harriet Tubman*, a book her father had given her when she was a child, the decades-old picture book became a source of inspiration. She said, "I felt like my freedoms had been taken away, with the pandemic and social injustice. The book was an impetus to do something, to act." She reached out to other women and formed We Walk With Harriet. The women gained national media attention and modeled a new image of Black women as not only strong but fit, and healthy.

We were dying disproportionately of COVID-19, but we were also challenging our traditional beliefs about what it means to be strong, reaching out to one another and finding community in places and spaces and in ways we could have never imagined before. Dr. Kanika Bell told me, "A lot of women are returning to therapy or going for the first time. We always see the pressure for Black women to embrace superhero roles, but I see a definite and intentional fight for many Black women to resist those unrealistic notions and practice radical self-care."

Another Mourning in America

"I was being pressured to stop crying and be strong."

—Diane Hawkins on the aftermath of the death of
her son Yusef Hawkins, who was beaten to death by a
White mob in Bensonhurst, New York, in 1985

As death closed in and he lay dying, struggling for breath, choking
beneath the knee of a White police officer, George Floyd whispered
for his mama with the words, "Mama. I'm through." "Mama," the
last word screamed or cried by soldiers dying on the battlefields of
America's Civil War, a word, according to linguists who have studied
the last days and hours of those nearing death, whose utterance in the
last moments of life is not uncommon. Mamie Till-Mobley, Saikou
Diallo, Sybrina Fulton, Gwen Carr, Geneva Reed-Veal, Larcenia
Jones Floyd, Tamika Palmer. What is the experience of grieving Black
mothers whose murdered children (Emmet Till, Amadou Diallo,
Trayvon Martin, Eric Garner, Sandra Bland, George Floyd, Breonna
Taylor) become fuel for public protests, indictments of official
violence, and occasionally actual changes in policy?

We think of grieving as a process that by its very nature is incremental
and private. And yet these women, who become in a sense every Black
mother, step forward, step out, stand up for their children. Black
mothers grieve for their children even before they die. We know, more
than many other mothers, how ravenous and insatiable death is, how it
lurks in our dreams, how it corrupts our reality. We hear its haunting

voice as the thread weaving the fabric of our lives, and especially of our children's lives. These women experience an exhausting swirl of emotions: Gratitude for the calls for justice and that their children have not been and will not be forgotten. Relief and release as the arms of the Black community, and sometimes the nation, enfold them. Anguish as their children's lives and past thoughts and deeds, dreams, and failings are pored over in the press and in social media for evidence of their culpability in their own demise.

Amadou Diallo didn't put his hands up fast enough. Trayvon Martin had smoked marijuana. Eric Garner had been arrested before. Sandra Bland talked back to the police officer who stopped her. George Floyd resisted arrest. Breonna Taylor's boyfriend shot in self-defense at unseen invaders who turned out to be police. Even in death, the reputations of the Black dead are tarnished with minutiae that reveal their humanity and complexity, but are translated as evidence that they deserved to die.

These mothers watch as their children are valorized and denigrated. They watch, and they step forward for morning talk-show interviews and marches in which they are suddenly activists and leaders of a throng that thinks they know and can feel their grief. They can't. These women become soldiers in a seemingly unwinnable war waged against them and their families. They form circles of support for themselves and others. They give themselves away and unto the nation and their communities and find in that surrender a form of salvation.

They are stoic. They become heroes. They are Strong Black Women. We ask that they perform their grief, not live it. Grief, which is a scramble of emotions, has to be offered up to us articulate, "respectable," well-dressed and well-rehearsed. We cannot offer them, even in these most soul-shattering moments, the space to howl. Our

grief has often been shackled. Mediated, censored. The bodies of
lynched men and women were left hanging publicly for days, and even
guarded by Whites to prevent Black families from claiming bodies
of loved ones. Our bodies still occupy both the public space and the
public imagination, and we are still struggling to claim them. When we
watch these grieving mothers, their defiance is magnificent. They write
books, run for public office, form foundations to support everything
from education to anti-police-violence efforts, dedicate the remainder
of their lives to lifting up and rescuing the memory of the lives of their
children. The message we give them is that they will be celebrated if
they are strong. They don't have the time for or the luxury of being
angry. But the anger is there. What are they doing with it? Where
is it going?

Black women, so often derided and characterized as angry, in these
moments which become not just a family reckoning but often a city
and a nation's reckoning with the results of violence and racism, offer a
marvelous grace to those willing to look into their faces. Faces that are
present at the placing of their children on the public altar of outrage
and activism. No one wants to go where these mothers now live and
breathe, and sleep and wake up, and seek silence and try to find words
and grasp for or shun God or do both at the same time. These women
are often still shell-shocked, the deaths raw and real but not real, the
hole where their center, their essence once was, that is gone, they fear,
never to return. In the activism, the speaking, the solidarity with all the
strangers who now have adopted their dead child as brother or sister,
there is a substance, something like earth, or soil, that fills the hole.
Then there comes a time when the longing for the darkened room, the
pastor's hand on a shoulder, the sound of grief, impolitely, overtakes
and overcomes everything else. Their child is calling, and they must
let that child go. They must return that child to the womb of memory.
There is life after death, and that child is still holding their hand.

Then there are the other mothers. Anonymous mothers. In truth, in painful truth, every street in America affirms that Black lives don't matter. Not even sometimes to Black people. There are so many ways to die in America. So many ways that are spectacular, planned expressions of rage and madness, like the killing of thirty-two school children at Sandy Hook Elementary School or the Stoneman Douglas High School shooting that left seventeen students dead. The awful grinding routine of death in violence-plagued neighborhoods continues in America's cities. No death is really routine, and our hearts break most when the victim is a child.

On the Fourth of July 2020, eleven-year-old Davon McNeal was shot and killed after an anti-violence cookout in Southeast Washington, DC. The youth was caught in the crossfire between rival gang members whose long-running feud had been the source of other violence in the community, the area with the city's highest homicide rate. Davon's mother Crystal McNeal is one of the city's violence interrupters, one of two dozen men and women embedded in twenty Washington, DC, communities whose job is to identify and stop conflict before it turns deadly. The killing and the hunt for the killers, who were quickly arrested, as well as the funeral for Davon, buried in his football jersey, clutching a football, received major coverage in the local media. The city mourned for Davon McNeal and his mother. I mourned for Davon and the three young men who had been arrested. I mourned for them and for their mothers. On a sultry July evening, nearing the end of a day dedicated to celebrating the ideas of liberty and freedom, those three young men ended the life of a child and stood to effectively lose a good portion of their futures if they were found guilty of murder. How had they become young men so devoid of compassion and concern for others that they would recklessly and easily hunt each other like prey on a street crowded with bystanders?

The narrative that quickly unraveled in the media was too easy, too neat. The tragedy of Davon's murder naturally and understandably superseded the tragedy of his killers. Labeled "gang members," which they apparently were, "felons," which they were, "repeat offenders," which they were, I wondered what had happened to them. They were not born with guns in their hands. I did not know much more information than I read about them in the *Washington Post* or heard on the local news. But there was a deeper, more complex knowledge— four mothers were now grieving. At the funeral for Davon, the neighborhood's City Council representative said, "If this doesn't shake the community and wake us up to do better for ourselves and our children, we may be lost forever."

To me, the words sounded like a mindless scolding of an errant child, not words to uplift a dispirited community. Crystal McNeal works to save her children and the children of others in a community that she knows is populated by too many people who have been "lost" to the economic and political powerbrokers (in a city that has had only African American mayors) for decades. The violence begets more violence because the root causes are never addressed. In the largely female-headed homes of Southeast, where the infant mortality rate is higher than in some Third World countries, where generational trauma (physical and sexual abuse) exists that has not been acknowledged or treated commensurate with the scale on which it occurs, where children are malnourished and experience food apartheid, there is well-deserved mistrust of police.

Yet, a self-defeating failure to work with the police to solve crimes ensures that the cycle of violence continues. Most of these young men's values have been shaped by an ideology of hyper- and toxic masculinity, beliefs they share with young White men in White supremacist gangs. They carry guns to protect themselves from real and imagined threats, to settle scores, and to be ready if someone they have victimized comes after them seeking revenge. Young men in gangs kill over a look, a word, presumed disrespect, because they have seen carnage in their neighborhoods, homes, and families unaddressed by a city in which they pay taxes on every bag of chips or soda they buy, taxes that flow out of their community, not into it. They see very little evidence that their Black lives, or the Black lives of their families, friends, and communities, matter. But those lives matter to many of us, and Crystal McNeal works to save people living in a Twilight Zone of neglect and isolation. Still, she could not save her own son.

Women in communities like these create the kinds of circles of support that "see them through." Neighbors, friends, and those dubbed "cousin," "brother," "sister" despite the absence of any biological link, form a chain of emotional comfort. Families are extended and extend themselves to encompass those who need help and those who can give help. These are not just violence-plagued communities; they are people-rich, intelligence-rich neighborhoods lacking opportunity for and investment in the residents.

Anonymous grieving Black mothers see heart-shaped balloons and teddy bears grace the site of their child's death in condolence. Or there will be a candlelit march through blood-stained streets. The families of the children of Sandy Hook Elementary School received $12.5 million in donations. In the aftermath of the Marjory Stoneman Douglas High School killings, a fund gave $400,000 to each of the families of the seventeen deceased students.

Those sums of money, which are a form of reparations, do the impossible and yet necessary: place a value on the life of the deceased, calculate their value to their families and society, how much money the young victims might have earned in a lifetime, estimate how much they would have contributed to their communities and the value of all of that. Life is priceless, but in America everything, even life, has a price. The incremental daily, frequently unreported and therefore "invisible" deaths of African Americans in America's cities often surpasses the combined deaths of Sandy Hook and Marjory Stoneman Douglas in a month.

Who is there to repair the souls of the mothers who are the backbone and the soul of communities where life is not cheap at all, but actually inordinately expensive? Do we know how to grieve? Black women, when they grieve, too often find themselves binding their own wounds in silence. Silenced by the manner in which we were prepared to live in America. The women of my generation were victims of, and many Black girls being raised today experience, corporal punishment. I remember how often my mother stifled my tears with the order, "Stop crying or I'll give you something to cry about." We have been taught and conditioned and threatened into silence.

Corporal punishment is not a unique expression of Black culture; rather it is an accommodation to the requirements of a racist society that has required families fearing for the safety of their children to "keep them in line" to avoid prison, arrest, a fatal encounter with police. That Black woman loudly scolding or brutally spanking her child in public screams "You're getting on my last nerve." Nerves are cells in the body that transmit information about feelings, actions, emotions. There is probably no more accurate cry of despair. That woman has literally exhausted the emotional energy required to consider and reflect. Her nerves are shot. When I have seen these public meltdowns, I hear not just the cries of the child being disciplined, but also the swallowed but still audible sobs of the mother. I see not a brutish monster, but a mother who needs help, probably on multiple levels. Keeping children in line suppresses the expression of anger, rage, and confusion. Silenced girls become silenced women. Black women have created a nurturing mythology of ourselves as able to speak truth to power, and tell it like it is, but we are deathly quiet about the pain in our hearts.

We see public displays and performances of Black women, bearing, carrying, managing, dealing with, holding up, overcoming, supporting, but not breaking. The story of how and why we break is undiscovered, taboo territory. What enters to fill the cavernous openings? Grief is much more than loss. It is acceptance, understanding, and transformation, and it is gaining another self, wounded and beautiful because of the scars. If Black women are masters at "maintaining," it is because they have so often been broken by grief.

Eve

Eve said that she had never before told her story, so much of it, nearly all of it, to another person. In the telling, she heard her girl voice, her young woman's voice, the voice of her motherhood, and the voice of the forty-two-year-old woman she has become. Now life is good. Whatever contentment means, whatever satisfaction is supposed to feel like, she's now being held aloft by its power. She has pulled herself, lifted, and propelled herself from ground beneath her feet that felt like quicksand. Pulled herself through years of darkness and uncertainty, her hands held by people who loved and believed in her. Pulled herself through years of grief.

A woman who for much of her life felt homeless, Eve has created in her apartment an atmosphere of peace, love, and stability. Once a week, she splurges on a bouquet of fresh flowers. Her days begin with prayer, offered up before her feet hit the floor.

She's looking for a house to buy. A house where she can create for
herself and her daughter a "forever home." She's a long way, but not
really so far, from the death, loss, and grief of her early years. Eve
has learned what no one ever taught her: To put herself first. To heal
herself first. To love herself first. Then, bolstered and courage-filled,
to give herself away and be nourished by what she gives and receives.
Sometimes her life feels like a dream. But Eve knows the sound and
smell and feel of nightmares she has spent many seasons running
from, and stumbling through, to arrive where she is now.

Hers is a hard story. From a hard time and place. Working-class and
poor 1980s and '90s Washington, DC, besieged by the drug wars. A
time and place where a generation of young Black men killed, or were
killed or imprisoned. Where the only work to be had in "the hood"
seemed to be satisfying the insatiable need of Americans, Black and
White, rich and poor, for an escape from their private hells. A time
and place where, despite the media images and even the reality of
neighborhoods drenched in blood, there were children, and there was
innocence, hope on those same streets.

"My father died six months before I was born. I was twelve when
my big brother was killed. A year later an uncle who was like a dad
to me died of a drug overdose. A couple of years later, the first boy
I thought I loved, a boy who told me he loved me, was killed by the
police. When I think about it or say it out loud, I remember wondering
if, somehow, I was the cause. If there was something about me that
caused their deaths.

"Our neighborhood in DC was rough. We had a troubled family life.
I was the youngest, after my sister Angelique and my brother Simon,
who was the oldest. Simon was more than a brother to me; he was
my protector. Because of all the trouble constantly going on in our

home when we were younger, Simon and I often stayed with my grandmother, who lived down the hall. There was my mom arguing with us kids, our stepdad arguing with us, her always taking his side, and so Simon and I just stayed with grandma. But my mother would eventually make us come back home.

"I was a bookworm, a tomboy. I was teased and bullied a lot. I was dark-skinned, skinny, and the kids at school and in the neighborhood called me everything but pretty. But Simon always took up for me, and I was always trailing him, following him around. By the time Simon was eighteen, he'd had enough of arguing with our stepfather, and he moved out and went to live with one of my mother's 'play sisters.' Her son was selling drugs, and soon Simon was too. They somehow got on the wrong side of Rayful Edmond, who controlled the drug trade in DC, and one night Simon and Jimmie were shot and killed by one of Edmond's crew. Shot at close range in the head, lying face-down on the street, they died instantly.

"Simon's death changed everything in the family, but we didn't talk about it. We didn't talk about our problems, never had, and now we talked even less. We all held our grief inside. I heard stories on the street about what had happened, and I actually learned more from the streets than at home. There were so many stories and so little truth. I hated the stories I was told about Simon. I was angry. My mom and sister were angry. But we just kept it all in. I hated being angry and I hated all the silence. Before Simon's death, I read voraciously. I was twelve, but had read the Bible from beginning to end. I played instruments. I didn't have many friends, but I had created my own little world through reading and books and my imagination, and the love of Simon and my grandmother. But after Simon was killed, I wasn't the same. I'd cry with my grandmother and she'd hold me, but she didn't know what to say either.

"Then, six months later, my father's brother died of an overdose. He had stepped in and stepped up because of my father's death and was always taking me places, the Children's Museum, Chuck E. Cheese. He knew I loved to read, so he'd buy me books. He was the neighborhood postman and, just like I had followed Simon, he let me follow him, walk with him while he delivered mail in the neighborhood. He had a good job, lived in the suburbs of Maryland, but had gotten addicted to crack and died of an overdose. There were kids in the neighborhood whose mothers or sisters were 'crack whores,' selling themselves for money to buy drugs. But Uncle Brad dying of crack? I couldn't believe it. I hadn't fully accepted or even understood Simon's death and now, a few months later, another loss. I resisted the idea that he was dead. I didn't really understand it. Then, because I was so upset, I wasn't allowed to attend the funeral. Another shock, but my mother and my sister, if they cried, I never saw it, and they threw themselves into their work and the message I got was that life goes on.

"My teenage years were hard. I was still carrying, almost like something I felt in my body, the deaths of my brother and uncle. I felt abandoned by my mother. She and my stepfather had split up and she was never around. She left the house at six a.m. to manage the cafeteria at a middle school and didn't come home most nights till ten. She wasn't present for me at all. My grandmother had moved in with us, and she was the only mother I knew. She cooked, cleaned, basically ran our house, and we were so close I slept in the bed with her.

"I began skipping school a lot. I was called ugly. Too Black. Poor. In those days there was so much violence in schools. If a group of girls didn't like you, they wanted to kill you. I saw the razors they hid in the corners of their mouths. Pretty soon, rather than go to school I'd spend the day downtown at the MLK branch of the library. I just figured let me be ugly by myself. I'd spend the day reading about Malcolm X or

Sojourner Truth or Maya Angelou. Some days I'd stay at home and read. My grandmother didn't homeschool me. She could barely read, but she covered for me when schools called to say I was absent.

"I was handling all this alone. There was the grief I was still carrying, and anger, and I felt like the school system had failed me. High school was no better. I attended five high schools in four years. I kept moving from school to school because of fights and violence and being bullied. My mother was missing in action and my grandmother was old and didn't know how to work the school bureaucracy, so I floated around the system on my own, filling out the needed forms and forging an adult's signature when needed. I was smart, well-read, had goals and ambitions, but nobody kept me on track, helped me make plans to realize them, and most of all, no one made me feel safe. By the time I turned seventeen, I was still in ninth grade because of all the time missed and being held back. So I dropped out and started working at KFC.

"When I met Jamal, I wasn't considered an ugly duckling anymore. I had started attracting sexual attention from men. But it made me uncomfortable, and always a little afraid. Jamal was a breath of fresh air. We met at a friend's apartment. He was my friend's cousin. While everyone else was sitting around playing bid whist and getting high, Jamal and I talked. He was a gangster, into the drug life, but he was the first guy I had met who I could talk to about the things I wanted, my thoughts and feelings, even some of the books I'd read. I could talk to him about all that right from the start. He had a big heart and was intelligent, thought about and talked about things that not a lot of guys I had met ever talked about—where he wanted to be in ten years, different countries he wanted to visit. He reminded me of my brother Simon. We got involved and I fell in love. I had never cared for a guy like that. Then his best friend got arrested and another one went missing. We broke up. I think he pulled away because he didn't want me around him if anything went down. Then we started talking again. My feelings had never changed. His hadn't either. The night he died, we had talked on the phone and he told me that he loved me and that he was getting out of the life.

"The thing you have to understand is that so many of the young men like Jamal, in another neighborhood, would've been headed to college. Many of them were smart enough for that, or if not college, maybe the military or trade school or something, anything more than selling drugs. They were drug dealers, but most of them weren't monsters. Most of them never shot anybody, but had to spend every day looking over their shoulder. I don't excuse the violence that some of them were involved in. How could I when my family paid such a high price? But looking back, I now see it was complicated. Way complicated. So when I got off the call that night, I felt relieved, like Jamal had a chance and that maybe we had a chance together. But a couple of hours later, when I paged him, someone called me back from his number and told me he'd been killed by the police.

"To this day, like with a lot of the deaths that happened on the streets, nobody who wasn't there really knew what had happened. It was January and he was walking down the street headed home and somebody called the police and said there was a man on the street with a gun acting funny. Somehow Jamal got shot in the back, killed by a cop. Seven police officers responded to the call. Jamal had turned eighteen the month before, in December. There was a routine investigation, but Jamal's death was ruled justified. His blood had seeped through the snow, and even though it snowed for a month after his death, every time I went by where it had happened, I could still see his blood. There were so many worst parts of Jamal's death, but one of the worst was that his parents, his friends, me, none of us really knew how he died, and we just had to accept that and go on living. But why would he tell me hours earlier that he wanted to get out of "the life" and live, and then act crazy with a gun? Was somebody stalking him? Was he about to go "missing" like his best friend?

"Now I was suicidal. I'd stand on the subway platform at Fort Totten and try to will myself to step in front of an oncoming train. They all came back to me, my father, my brother, my uncle, and now Jamal. All the grief for each of them. All the anger for each of them. And I was convinced in some way they had died because of me. And I hated the police. I was filled with so much grief and anger and hate, some days I could just barely get out of bed. And once again, nobody around me could help me say out loud what I needed to say and what I was afraid to say. My mother was still absent emotionally. My sister, like me, had never expressed the things that our family decided had to be hidden. My grandmother's love, as deep as it was, wasn't enough to make me feel healed in any way.

"I loved Jamal for a long, long time after he was killed. I think I was still loving him when I was with most of the guys I was with for years. I know I was still in love with him when I got pregnant with my daughter. Every guy I was with had to look at Jamal's framed picture in my bedroom. My daughter's father was just like me, young, and lost, so when I told him I was pregnant, I didn't ask for anything and he didn't offer anything. Because of all of the chaos I'd known, I wanted my child to never know any of that. I had wanted to die and now I had a reason to live. I was going to be somebody's mother. So I had to be somebody. So I attended night school and got a GED and then enrolled at Prince Georges Community College. I had to figure out a way to make something of my life. I was a single mother. I was lucky that my grandmother helped me with my daughter. In between classes I worked at whatever I could—security guard, waitress, telemarketing.

Then a part of me realized I was a mother, but I was still young, and I wanted to be and act young. So there was the school, work, mommy track, and the party-good-time track.

"I was doing all these things, juggling all this, and drinking and smoking marijuana when I was with my friends because it made me feel good and it made me forget everything I didn't want to remember. I think I was scared to feel the kind of love I had with Jamal again, so for a long time, over a decade, I was in and out of impossible relationships, relationships that couldn't last, relationships that in a way I didn't want to last. But I still wanted to be somebody, to have something to show for my life.

"So a couple of years after I graduated from the community college, I enrolled at the University of the District of Columbia and majored in business. My daughter was getting older, and the older she got the more pressure, good pressure, I felt to be more and do more. I was in a fog, but it felt like it was clearing a little more every day.

"I have to say that, as someone who felt let down by my family, I was inspired by the family of one of my girlfriends. There were people in that family who I could talk to about what I wanted to do with my life, people who encouraged me and said they believed in me. When my grandmother died, I went over to my friend's grandmother's house and cried and told her I didn't have a grandmother anymore. This woman went into the kitchen, made me a plate of food, placed it in front of me, and said, "You have a grandmother now." That family was like a light in a really dark place for me.

"It felt good to be back in school again, surrounded by all the things I had always wanted to have when I was in school as a kid. I finally had all the books I could ever want to read, teachers who rewarded me for being smart, classrooms with other people who saw learning as a way to build a good life. Every year the stakes were getting higher, my daughter was getting older, and I was somehow getting stronger.

"The turning point came when my daughter and I graduated in the same year. She graduated from high school and I graduated from college, something we had both decided she was going to do. I got an administrative job with the DC government. I decided that, from now on, I was in charge. I started to do what I had never really done— assessed and looked at my life, looked at it almost like it belonged to someone else. I became very reflective and felt myself at a crossroads. I took a deep breath. I started running to get physically strong. I started eating healthy and I talked with my daughter about my traumas, how I'd grown up in a family of silence and pain. I told her I'd always love and support her, no matter what. I told her that her feelings weren't anything to be ashamed of or afraid of.

"When my daughter was still quite young, I fell into a deep depression and tried to kill myself. I was hospitalized in the psych ward at Washington Hospital Center and for a week I was on suicide watch. They sent me home with the name of a therapist to schedule a session with. It didn't help. I was really afraid to open up because, if I did, if I told the therapist how out of control I really felt, my daughter would be taken from me. The first session, the therapist made me feel worse, and in the second session she suggested I go to church as an answer to my problems. I never went back. Maybe if I had stayed with it, tried to find another therapist, my road would have been easier. But I was a poor Black woman and I felt the system and even those who were supposed to help me had labeled me. As not a good mother, as not worth saving.

"I'm at peace but I'm not finished. There's a lot of 'stuff' between me and my mom, a lot of anger, and I keep my distance. I regret that my daughter has no relationship with her father. Just like me, but for different reasons. I read a book once about women who never knew their fathers or had distant relationships with them. The author called it 'daddy hunger.' I still have some of that, and I am sure my daughter will as well. But she can be whole and happy despite that. I will always love Jamal, but I've let him go. I'm a work in progress. These days, when I think about my life, I think not just about all those deaths that kept coming, but the good people and the good things that kept coming too. I think about my own strength and how I made it this far and that I know I can go the rest of the way too."

When I asked Dr. Pamela Brewer her thoughts about the challenges of grieving for Black women, her answer was comprehensive and compassionate. I wanted to give her the last word.

"We as a society tend to censor the grieving process. Employers are certainly known to put very specific limits on who to grieve and when to grieve and for how long. When it comes to Black women, it can be even more curtailed at the hands of colleagues and employers and even ourselves. Often, as Black women grieve, they are seen as overreacting, making an excuse to take time off from work, while a White woman could be well supported to take as much time as necessary. This is particularly the case when the cause of the grief is considered appropriate, for example, an illness or addiction that is deemed acceptable or understandable, or violence that is not blamed on the victim.

"For a Black woman, however, the response, the compassionate embrace so needed at a time of grief, is often not available. If the cause of the grief is seen as socially unacceptable (murder, murder by police, drug/addiction/poverty-related, or 'her fault'), there can be a particularly smaller pool of understanding and acceptance from which to draw support.

"What is also true, and often overlooked, is that as Black women we experience small and large loss/grief episodes as part of our daily experience. Socially, politically, economically, professionally, educationally, financially—loss, grief, it's the daily lens through which we work to squeeze out some semblance of a healthy life, despite the daily grind of loss. When that grief is exacerbated by the loss of a loved one, regardless of how 'close' that loved one is, the grieving process is so much more complex.

"For Black women, the loss of another Black body, a close one or a person miles away, is so enveloping, often overwhelming, sadly so commonplace, that there can be an instinctive tendency to shut it down/wall it off/do the 'Strong Black Woman' dance in order to continue the daily duties of life. And isn't that traumatic learning, what we learned through our ancestors' lives? A way to survive was to put the pain in a box and continue to work. Because truly, to let in the horror of it all was to/is to take one's breath away. But when we don't let our grief in, allow it to be felt in the kaleidoscope of ways in which we feel, when we do not allow ourselves the gift of healthy grieving and we try to send the grief underground—it simply rests on another layer of grief, yet unresolved. It is very hard for a wound to heal when it is continually reopened. And we continue to hurt. Ourselves and those around us.

"Are there spaces in our community to authentically grieve? For those of us who have that 'good girlfriend' or circle of girlfriends, or even a close male friend, there can be tremendous solace. But then again, the myths of grieving ('you just need to get over it,' 'it's been XX months,' 'it's time for you to move on,' 'you are young, you can have another,' and so much more that people often unknowingly express or say or believe), along with what is often the reality of daily life, often force Black women in particular to grieve when there is time, and often, too often, that time is never found... So we must find it, create [it], in whatever amazing and creative ways work for us. Including setting limits. Take a ridiculously long shower, take a break from all your devices—you know how to figure it out. Creating 'talking circles' can be helpful and healing and freeing and empowering, all at the same time. Particularly during the process of grieving, it is important to treat ourselves as we would a dear friend—someone we love and care about, someone we treasure."

Say My Name

"*I just think, you know, the biggest superheroes we've ever had have been Black women who have looked at a set of conditions that are designed for them to fail and designed to kill them and said, we're going to live anyway. And not only are we going to live—we're going to thrive.*"

—Brittany Cooper, author of *Eloquent Rage: A Black Feminist Discovers Her Superpower*

The atmosphere in the room was fraught with tension and dissatisfaction. A cloud had settled over English Department faculty meetings over the past several weeks, as reasonable discussion curdled into argument and fractious debate. We were trying to decide between two candidates for a position in the university's MFA Graduate Creative Writing Program. Specifically, we were looking at candidates to fill a vacancy in the poetry program. The women enrolled in the program had thrown down a gauntlet, delivered with determination and emotion to the chair of the department. Since the program's founding, the faculty had never included a female poet. It was time to rectify the situation. The department's search committee had narrowed the choice down to two highly and equally qualified candidates, one male, one female, both White.

Women poets in the program, getting wind of the final candidates, had begun lobbying in favor of the respected, award-winning female poet, then resident at a Midwestern college. A decision that appeared to me to be straightforward and overdue had become bogged down in resistance from male faculty who sniffed the dreaded odor of

affirmative action. The poetry program had maintained a faculty of
two, and the remaining poet had launched a fierce campaign for the
equally respected award-winning male poet, who was an old friend.
At a previous meeting, the program's remaining poet noisily entered
the small faculty lounge, pushed his chair between two other faculty
at the crowded table and dramatically tossed his friend's resume, all
sixty pages (he loudly informed us), into the center of the bruised, dull
wooden conference table, announcing as the papers slid, almost as
though planned, right in front of the Department Chair, "This is who
we should hire, and this is who I will vote for."

As theatrical as this exhibition was, it was rather tame. I had watched
shouting matches, meltdowns, loud diatribes, patronizing lectures, as
a regular and expected and, it came to seem, required part of English
Department faculty meetings. Often it was the White guys who lapsed
into sarcasm, whiney complaint, and loud condescension in defense
of a shift in department requirements, consideration of a new major,
course loads, class size, committee assignments, and responsibilities.
Women, even when passionate, were studied, polite, looking everyone
in the eye. Making a point but never endeavoring to transgress.

Several years before I joined the faculty, after half a dozen Black faculty
were denied tenure in a two-year period and the Black Student Union
complained not only to the then-president, but the media and the
local NAACP, the tenure process was reviewed and restructured. I
was one of two Black women in the department and was a tenured
full professor teaching Fiction and Nonfiction in the MFA Graduate
Creative Writing Program.

As this meeting began to wind down, it was clear that after several
weeks of discussion, everyone knew where everyone stood on the two
candidates. I supported the female poet. But no one knew where the

Department Chair stood. Arguments that had been made weeks earlier for either poet kept bubbling up, filling the room with an insistent undercurrent. In an effort to quell the brewing verbal disorder, the Chair announced, "Everything you all have said will be taken into consideration. But you all remember what happened the last time we hired a woman."

A silence, full-blown and complete, dissolved the cloud of tension, and it seemed that I could not hear anyone breathing or making a sound. *You all remember what happened the last time we hired a woman.* The words didn't just fill my ears, they stopped my heart. Was I the last woman hired? I quickly wondered. Feverishly calculating the odd math of "diversity hiring," I realized that I wasn't considered a woman hire, but a Black hire. Nonetheless, I was stunned. I quickly gazed at my colleagues, shifting in their chairs, sharing meaningful gazes that spoke what it was clear no one was prepared to say. No one except me.

I was sitting three seats away from the Chair, on his left. I, calmly at first, asked if he meant what he said and, without waiting for an answer, told him that I was deeply offended by the comment, which had objectified, demonized, and trivialized women candidates. I spoke with emotion, shook my head in disbelief, my voice nearly cracking. I am sure my response, which was emotional, articulate, rational, and clear, lasted only sixty seconds or so, but its force and how unexpected it was, how I had broken the rules of female participation in these meetings, made it feel as though it lasted an hour. The Chair, with whom I had an easy, comfortable relationship, looked at me, said nothing, and then ended the meeting. As everyone rose to leave the room, I was still shaking from both his words, which had felt like a physical assault, and my own rage.

I had seen myself as standing up for women. I had my own "Ain't I A Woman?" moment. If I was going to speak against sexism or racism, I had to speak when and where it happened. When and where it entered the room. A quiet conversation with the Chair after the meeting in his office would not allow me to do what was called for in that moment. To bear witness to an alternative vision of who all the women in that room were. Whatever we were, we were not a mistake, a problem, an error. As I left the meeting and walked back to my office, I recalled the White female faculty members who I had seen leaving the Chair's office in tears, how I had heard their complaints about his verbal insensitivity toward them. I had never experienced any of that, and in the aftermath of my own display of indignation at an expression of blatant sexism (Angry Black Woman 101, in the eyes of my colleagues), not one of those White female faculty approached me to discuss what I had viewed as my defense of them and of me. It would be weeks before I realized that, to them, I wasn't a sister in the feminist struggle. I was Black woman, a breed apart from them. And that, as such, they had no need for to me to fight what they saw as their battle. Especially if they chose not to fight it themselves.

Later in the afternoon, the Chair knocked on my office door and apologized. I had no knowledge of what had ensued after the last "female hire" and didn't want to know, but I told him that whatever had happened, I felt it was sexist and unfair to taint the current search with such a statement. His apology seemed sincere. I told him "apology accepted" and lapsing into comforting woman mode; I assured him that the process of filling this position had all our nerves a bit rattled and I was certain that the comment was not evidence of his real feelings. It appeared that, at the conclusion of that meeting, the Chair was leaning toward the male poet, but he subsequently decided to offer the position to the well-respected, award-winning Midwestern female poet.

In every academic community I have been a part of, I have sought community. The isolation of the Black faculty experience at historically White institutions makes the search for community an exercise often in near despair. In the MFA program at that university, although I had published a well-received memoir and two novels, I was rarely sought out as a thesis director by the graduate students I taught with my White male colleague in the fiction program. While the university, in an effort to "diversify" the faculty, hired me to fill the fiction slot after the departure of a prominent female writer from the Caribbean, in the program itself, as a Black woman, I was marginalized and "Mammified." Students often asked me to intercede on their behalf with White male faculty they were afraid to approach, as though I were the head of human resources and not a professor of creative writing.

"If I get on his bad side now, he could ruin my career," I was told by White students about disputes with White male faculty. These were White graduate students who had already claimed and envisioned careers they feared could be ruined, years later, by the ire of a ticked-off professor. I became their go-to person as they attempted to draft me to fix or repair damaged relationships with White male faculty. Never once did I accept the thankless job offer.

Despite my publication record; my literary activism, which had helped to create a national literary organization that had created more publishing opportunities for Black writers; my sincere and compassionate interest in the students in the program as people, not only as writers; for most of the White students, I was deemed of little use to them. They simply could not imagine that I could advance their careers in any way. My class evaluations were excellent, my relations with the students friendly, warm, and cordial, but one young woman who led the push for hiring a female poet told me in my office one day

that many of the students in the program were "afraid of" me. She told
me this in the sympathetic, privileged voice of liberal Whiteness, told
me this for my own good, so I would understand their hesitancy to
have me direct their thesis work.

This young woman and I stayed in touch after I left the program. I
liked a lot of things about her. However, I knew what she was really
saying. *Translation:* I was a Black woman who was smart, talented,
accomplished, spoke my mind, didn't feel that I had to follow the
social rules of the program, and I had incited in many of the students
a mix of awe and fear. Their racial anxieties led then to question my
competence, and, in the questioning, the problem became me, not
their own racism.

For the small handful of students in the program who requested that
I work with them on their thesis, I was coach and mentor, advising
them as they completed a substantial portion of a novel, a short story
collection, or a memoir as the culmination of their three years in the
program. Unspoken and unacknowledged was the preference of most
of these White thirty-something writers to work on their cherished
projects with someone who they could see themselves one day being.
Someone they felt they could instinctively trust as qualified. Not
someone who looked like me.

Despite "performing" satisfaction when I was far from that in such
a racially toxic environment, by the time I claimed my "Ain't I A
Woman?" moment in that faculty meeting, I knew who I was. It didn't
matter that I was undervalued. I was Marita Golden, and I was tenured.
I possessed a full-fledged, certified, and approved voice that I could
use. I had lunch once a semester with the university's Black provost,
a woman who thirty years earlier had been denied admission to this
university because of segregation, while the state of Virginia paid for

her to attend a university in Boston. The president of the university had signed off on a contract between the university and the Hurston/ Wright Foundation that promised logistical and financial support of the foundation's programs. I had been hired to make a difference, and I would do that wherever and however I could. I didn't mind being an Angry Black Woman in the eyes of others, often on slow burn, sometimes on simmer. Anger was my fuel, it was high-grade, a hybrid mix of intolerance for bullshit and joy at what that brew could bring forth in the world. I had learned which battles to fight, and to fight them from a fortified position.

I am mad about injustice, but I am not a Mad Black Woman. I don't suffer fools, but I'm not a "Sapphire." Both the Angry Black Woman and the Sapphire labels are racist caricatures of the most admirable qualities of Black women, our willingness to, in the words of Congressman John Lewis, make "good trouble," and our desire to fight for our rights. The Angry Black Woman and Sapphire are evil twins composed of the material of White supremacist hatred and lies. They live in our heads, censor our actions, and force us to second-guess our natural instincts. They police us and induce a kind of schizophrenia that splits us into warring versions of ourselves. You can measure the progress of Black women by how often and how regularly they are labeled angry, mean, bitch. Redefine the game of tennis, become First Lady, become a US senator, a vice-presidential candidate, and in the public square, you may never be called by your name again. White working-class voters who out of "anger and a sense of marginalization" voted for Donald Trump were recipients of apologies and hand-wringing, anguished mea culpas in mainstream media in the aftermath of the 2016 election. *Why weren't they listened to? Why were they silenced? What can we do to start hearing their voices now?* asked the headlines. The Democratic Party turned itself inside out scrambling to get the votes of people who had not voted Democratic since Lyndon Johnson lost the South when he signed into law a series of Civil Rights Acts. But when Black women politicians forthrightly state the case of the continuing need for racial redress, the message from some quarters is, "Why can't you move on?"—from others, "Shut up."

We are complicit in the crime. African American culture, through folklore, cinema, music, and our special brand of comedy, has long adopted and reinforced many of these stereotypes, as Black men negotiate their own mixed and mired feelings about Black female agency and autonomy. Black men and women are avid and loyal consumers of media that presents offensive and dangerous Black women tropes—tropes often embedded in some version of the Strong Black Woman prototype. But how did these women take up residence in our hearts and minds?

The answer is found in the long, sorry story of enslavement and fear of the power and genius of Black men and women. After the end of slavery, we were not re-enslaved only by peonage, sharecropping, Black codes, lynching, and segregation. We were re-enslaved as books and articles and theses written by White scholars at the country's most prestigious universities, and vaudeville, and minstrel shows, and every form of cultural expression was marshalled to continue as during slavery, arguing that Black men were both savage, maniacal, bloodthirsty criminals and ignorant buffoons, and that we might be free in body but we would never control the essence of our image. Black women were portrayed as servile Mammies whose job was to solve White folks' problems, and simultaneously as emasculating shrews.

This national initiative has never stopped to catch its breath. Every generation of Americans has been fed some version of this poisonous mythology. Careers have been made on it. Actors Black and White have become famous bringing the myth to life. Among the most loyal and avid consumers of programs and films that demean us are Black folk. Overrepresented by comedies, that imbalance implies that our lives are a barrel of laughs, that we are suited, not for nuanced drama, but for one-dimensional comedy. The power of media—TV, film, literature, videos, social media—to shape our image of ourselves, to encode expectations, aspirations, and actions, is monumental.

Watching *Amos 'n' Andy*, I learned what a Black woman was. She was the wife of Kingfish, a get-rich-quick con man. The show was created by two White actors who originally played Amos and Andy on the radio from 1928 to 1960. For thirty-two years, Americans of all races tuned in to hear the ridiculous malapropisms of Kingfish—"I deny the allegation, your honor, and I resents the alligator"—the sheer stupidity of his friend Andy, who week after week Kingfish bamboozled, and the shrieking anger of Sapphire. The show was the first TV show with an all-Black cast, airing from 1951 to 1953 on CBS, with syndicated reruns from 1954 to 1966. It was finally removed after years of agitation by the NAACP and the pressures of a growing civil rights movement. But by then a whole generation of Black girls like me had grown up under the show's influence.

In another world, Sapphire would be portrayed as an enforcer of morality, ethics, and fair play, a woman urging her deadbeat husband to become a better man. But because she was merely a Strong Black Woman on overdrive, she was annoying and frightening. She was someone no Black woman wanted to be.

Sapphire greeted me in some incarnation on nearly every Black situation comedy. She could be middle-aged, like the maid Florence on *The Jeffersons*, or old, like Aunt Esther on *Sanford and Son* in the seventies, or young, like Pam on *Martin* in the nineties—shows in perennial rotation on cable networks. As the new century dawned, she could be openly called and even claim the title of "reigning bitch," like Omarosa Manigault on *The Apprentice,* the women of *The Real Housewives of Atlanta*, and the tabloid talk shows. Black women were making bank, laughing all the way *to* the bank. The portrayal of Black women on all these programs was and is contested and critiqued, but the power of this presentation that adapts itself to every new media form, from Facebook to Instagram, is relentless. Those raging, crazed women, the fear that we are them, the fear that we could melt down and become them, is ever present. Even the groundbreaking show *Black-ish* reinforces the Sapphire/Black bitch syndrome. The twin Diane, who is also the darkest-complexioned of all the actors, is portrayed as vindictive, unforgiving, scheming. She is a little Sapphire.

Media hijacks, hypnotizes us, socializes us, tells us who we are and should be. Too many media representations of Black women undercut the effort to create and maintain mental health. Negative images aren't just benign "images"; they seep into and blur our vision of ourselves. We have to recognize harmful representations, challenge them, and counteract their impact. And we have to talk with our sisters, mothers, daughters, and female and male kin about what we see and its effect, powerfully positive as well as damaging.

Those young Black female students at the University of Virginia who swallowed dissent when confronted with classroom racism had never watched *Amos 'n' Andy*, but they feared "Sapphire" was a mutation dormant in their bloodstream. They had grown up watching her sisters and cousins on the shows that "raised" them. *The Cosby Show* and its spin-offs presented an entirely different vision of Black womanhood—respectable, smart, capable. But Sapphire lurked everywhere. Seen and unseen. If they gave in even for a momentary lapse of honesty, they feared they would morph into some Black Female Incredible Hulk and they would lose all legitimacy in the White world. We have to learn how to say our own names.

We have to own our anger and create ways in the classroom, the living room, the workplace, to say what we need to say. Or our silence will kill us. Anger is too powerful, too righteous, too replenishing, and too nurturing to have it stolen from us. But anger is where we start. It is the spark; creativity, insight, and intelligence are the flame.

Say Your Name

It's Black History Month and you are the one Black person in your American history class, and you are female. The students turn to you for answers. You have the right to remind the class and the teacher that slavery didn't just happen to African Americans and that you would like to discuss how White Americans were impacted by enslaving people or living in a society that did. Black history is American history. Suggest little-known but remarkable Americans who contributed to America's growth for discussion and exploration. Suggest discussion of White abolitionists alongside Harriet Tubman. This may unsettle Black and White folks, but it will make them think.

You are overwhelmed, unsupported. You work eight hours on your job and then another eight or more at home as cook, maid, psychiatrist. You are seething with frustration. Near breakdown. You feel unseen, unappreciated. Call a family meeting and ask for help. Remind everyone that the family is a unit, a system that requires the input, action, and support of all who are part of it and benefit from it. Jointly create a system of assignments. Say that everyone will be held accountable. Their reward is a home in which they all are invested, a home in which everyone is respected and valued.

A watershed moment in my journey to New Age Strong Black Woman occurred when my husband was diagnosed with lymphoma, a cancer that he fought successfully. But the journey to remission was fraught with challenges for us both. I was caretaker, chauffeur, as well as soulmate, wife, and friend. I had spiritually claimed his healing, and yet the emotional and physical demands of caring for him were often more than I could bear. I felt lonely, isolated. I missed the intimacy and closeness that had been curtailed as he fought to marshal his strength, to recover from the chemotherapy and radiation that halted the cancer's growth. The drugs he took for treatment sometimes altered his personality, making him unrecognizable. I cried silently many nights, and despite my omnipresence in Joe's life, felt invisible and erased. When his family called daily to inquire about Joe, I seethed in anger that no one ever asked about me. Finally, one evening, I broke down and told my mother-in-law that I felt that no one in the family appreciated the burden I was carrying. Why, I asked, did no one ever ask about me? The family responded immediately, not only with expressions of concern, but with inquiries about what I needed and what they could do to help. Their transformed attitude made the final months of treatment more manageable. And I felt seen and valued. Because I had asked to be seen and valued. Because I said to myself, "The hell with being strong, I am hurting and the people I love need to know it."

On your job, you are underpaid, discriminated against, denied promotion. Be strategic. Save emails, take notes that include dates, names, meetings, quotes, and conversations. Create a proposal for advancement that allows your "boss" to see possibilities for her elevation or enhancement along with yours. Still stuck? Seek emotional support and advice from trusted friends, a professional, or, if you need to, a lawyer. Get clear about what you actually need and desire. Find it or create it.

African American women are geniuses at creative and sophisticated use of anger. We use it slyly like Beyoncé. With forthrightness and conviction like Maxine Waters. With elegance and authenticity like Michelle Obama. Soulfully like Aretha Franklin. Eloquently like Toni Morrison. Wickedly like Moms Mabley. Brilliantly like my sisters in academia, scholars creating a revolutionary new canon of ideas about our history and experience. Subversively, like the sound of a female elder's wisdom.

Becoming a New Age Strong Black Woman Means...

Honoring the ways that Black women's anger has inspired action, activism, and change. I love my Black woman anger and cherish it as a force that has protected our children and families, stood by our men, fought for health and safety in our communities, and pushed our country over and over again into the fulfillment of its promise and the contract it made with all its citizens. I am proud to be angry when I need to be. Because Black women have a long history of using anger strategically to achieve long-term goals.

Healing Stories

"Storytelling was the first opportunity for Black folks to represent themselves as anything other than property."

—Virginia Hamilton, author of *The People Could Fly*

"Every book, every volume…has a soul. The soul of the person who wrote it and of those who read it and lived and dreamed with it. Every time a book changes hands, every time someone runs his eyes down its pages, its spirit grows and strengthens."

—Carlos Ruiz Zafón

"A writer's life and work are not a gift to mankind, they are its necessity."

—Toni Morrison

I didn't grow up in a house filled with books, yet I learned from my parents that stories were a force for healing. My father told me stories of heroes and heroines of a glorious Black past that was much more than slavery and that lasted much longer than four hundred years. It was in my father's taxi, or sitting on the back porch with him in the summer, drinking a glass of lemonade, or as he tucked me into bed at night, that I received my first lessons in Black history. By the time I was twelve, I knew the names J. A. Rogers, a Jamaican American journalist and historian who wrote over a dozen books about the

African diaspora, including *Africa's Gift to America* and *The World's Great Men of Color*, and George Washington Williams, the author of the first multi-volume history of African Americans, published in the late nineteenth century.

My father equipped me for a world in which my fifth-grade Washington, DC, class would be confidently informed by a White teacher that "the slaves were happy working on the plantations." His stories inspired me when I heard those words to quickly raise my hand and, when I was called on, to inform the teacher that "My father told me that the slaves didn't want be slaves and wanted to be free."

Long before I knew I was wounded, my father was healing me with stories. He healed himself every time he told them. My father was a great storyteller, with his deep voice, and the measured, mannered way he used his body to enhance even the most thrilling narrative. My father, it seemed to me, loved to tell stories, more than anything else, about Black people.

I was a voracious, avid reader as a child, and my parents joked that I would read a matchbook cover with fascination. In my school days I read a lot of books, among them, Nancy Drew, the biography of Helen Keller, *Charlotte's Webb, Little Women, A Tale of Two Cities*, and *War and Peace* in high school on my own. But none of those stories healed me like my father's oral narratives of the ambitious visionaries who peopled and propelled the history of African peoples.

My father carried those stories with him like a fingerprint. I always felt they were in his flesh, palpable and alive. It was from my father, not a teacher in school, that I first heard the names Frederick Douglass, Sojourner Truth, Hannibal, Toussaint L'Ouverture, and George Washington Carver. These people lived not only in my father's memory from books he had read and stories he had been told, but also in the world we both inhabited, with every breath he took. My father was able to live and dream because of those stories. Stories that informed him that he was more than a second-class citizen in a second-rate democracy. Those stories were ritual, binding me to my father and to the historical figures that his stories told me I was kin to. It was from my father that I learned more about American history and facts about presidents than I would ever be taught in school.

My father was always "schooling" me, and told me residents of the city of Washington, DC, couldn't vote and had no representation in Congress because of its large Black population. He created a world that felt, to him, beyond the reach of the White man. I often think that, in a world not constricted by segregation and racism, my father could have and would have occupied a stage as large as the heroes he made real for me. It wasn't the size of the life you lived that was most important, he felt, but who you thought you were in that life, no matter how big or small it felt or seemed to be.

If my father's stories informed me that my racial legacy was complex, long, and populated by figures who deserved movies and books about their lives, my mother's stories were intimate and aspirational. My parents had been born to a long line of optimists. Black people whose faith in the internal engine of history and the justice of the fight for racial equality convinced them that the futures of their children would inevitably be characterized by ever-growing expressions of the full meaning of the nation's founding documents. Like most Americans, my parents could have recited little from the Declaration of Independence except "All men are created equal."

My parents never quibbled over the fact that the authors of the Declaration were in large part enslavers whose bold assertion was not meant for our ancestors or their progeny. They knew what I would learn firsthand when I became the writer they prepared me to be. First and foremost, the founders were writers, imagining and codifying in language their vision of a new world. A writer is mostly a channel to bring a story into the world that belongs ultimately and most completely to those who read it, hear of it, memorize it, and read into it who they are or who they want to become.

"You're going to write a book one day," my faith-filled mother told me. For my eighteenth birthday, she gave me a subscription to the *New York Times*, and she talked about my love of books and writing to her friends as though they were evidence of a talent that could part the waters and raise the dead. Using imagination, faith, and the evidence of my predilections that she witnessed every day, my mother created a future-oriented healing story about who I was going to be that transcended all the limitations she saw around her. Her stories, combined with those of my father, became a magic carpet I rode in my mind. My destination was a world built on the foundation of the heroes in my father's stories and my mother's charge to me. A world whose doors I would open and stride through because they told me I could.

When I began writing my first book, a memoir, *Migrations of the Heart*, my life appeared to me to be one of dashed hopes, puzzle pieces, jagged edges, and grief. The book is the story of my coming of age against the backdrop of the cultural and political change of the 1960s and my marriage to a Nigerian, the four years I lived in Nigeria, and my return to the US after the marriage failed. That is the

plotline, but the book is really a story of identity, finding your voice
and your place in the world. Writing facilitated my healing from a
painful separation and divorce. Writing about my life, I discovered its
meaning and its magnitude. I had to pore over memory, recollection,
experience, and invest it with significance. I had to shatter myth,
uncover secrets, take a deep breath, and give it color and shape. As
I wrote, I resurrected my dead parents and got to love them all over
again, confront and question them. As I wrote in service to a story that
I envisioned as literature, I revisited my motives, extended compassion
in place of bitterness, and viewed my life not as wreckage, but as
art. Simultaneously beautiful and imperfect, art unfolds throbbing
with uncertainty and offering the promise that you can call it home.
Writing about my parents, I learned how they had loved me and how
I had loved them. Writing about myself, I found out what I was made
of. The stories that are the most painful can offer the largest realm
of healing.

According to science, one reason the brain falls in love with a good
story is because hearing and reading stories releases the hormones
oxytocin and cortisol. Oxytocin is a hormone that regulates empathy
and social interaction. Cortisol is connected to the stress response.

When a story introduces a likeable character facing a difficult problem,
oxytocin causes the brain to empathize with the character's situation,
and cortisol causes the brain to feel stress over the character's problem.
These reactions lead the reader, listener, or viewer to become invested
in the character's plight.

Stories, because of their imaginative power, have much greater impact than simple facts. Increased brain engagement leads not only to increased thought on the engaging topic, but increased memory as well. When that engagement and memory are controlled and focused in a positive way, the brain's love for storytelling can be the key to healing and happiness.

I asked Black women who love to read how stories have healed them.

"I read Breath, Eyes, Memory *by Edwidge Danticat after my therapist, an Afro-Puerto-Rican woman, reached over and pulled it from her bookshelf during our session. She wasn't giving it to me, but letting me hold it in my hands, take in the picture of the young Haitian author and read the blurb about an immigrant girl, Sophie Caco, who like me struggled with a history of sexual violence and how to reconcile her relationship with her mother after many years of separation when her mother left Haiti to live in America.*

"I immediately bought my own copy of the novel and devoured it. I paid special attention to Sophie's struggles in Haiti during her separation from and longing for her mother. That mirrored my longing for my mother after she left Jamaica for the United States. I too desperately wanted to connect with a mother who seemed more distant after we were reunited.

"I followed Sophie's reverse journey with trepidation and wonder. She ran away from her husband and returned to Haiti to her grandmother and aunt with her baby daughter, to talk, to take in, to process at a deeper level the trauma that her deeply wounded mother had perpetrated on her in a misguided effort to keep her safe. I believe my therapist handing me that novel signaled that she had the kind of cultural capital that prepared her to support me as I made my own deep dive into my own history of trauma. Sophie's fearlessness helped me to understand that I had the strength to undertake a similar journey toward healing and liberation from the pain of the past."

—Jacqueline Samuda

"I had already experienced a divorce, and now, four years later, I was at the end of another relationship. For a second time, I found myself packing up my son and moving out of a home I thought was forever, to uncertainty and loneliness. I scolded myself for failing once again at love. I was defeated, angry, and most of all, in pain. When I opened the pages of All About Love: New Visions by bell hooks, I found salvation. In the preface she writes, 'We can find the love our hearts long for, but not until we let go of grief about the love we lost long ago, when we were little and had no voice to speak the heart's longing.' In her words, I found release from my negative mind, comfort that I wasn't alone. I was reassured that I was worthy of love—from others, but mostly from myself."

—Melanie Hatter

"When Tony got shot, no one could console me. The news said, 'gang war.' That was impossible. Tony wasn't in a gang. He was a cool young brother from the neighborhood. Growing up Black on the South Side of Chicago during the late sixties, I was well acquainted with gang violence, but getting blasted off the planet was new. Books could always set me straight, pick me up when I was in a funk, or put me in a headspace of hope and happy endings. But now my favorites, Laura Ingalls and Nancy Drew, left me hollow and even cynical at thirteen-and-a-half years old. There were no 'Tonys' in their stories. What did they know?

"My parents handed me a book called The Soul Brothers and Sister Lou. I blinked twice at seeing a sweet-faced Black girl gracing the cover wearing two ponytails on her head, just like mine. It was the weekend. Swaddling myself in my comforter, my bed became my bunker until the book was finished. It didn't disappoint. Louretta (Lou), the main character, was me and she wasn't me. Her life was hard, and mine wasn't. But the central theme of life in America for Black girls our ages sizzled on those pages as if my hand had written them. I saw my friends, the South Side families from the neighborhood…and I saw Tony all over those pages. This book was home for me. I never read another Laura Ingalls or Nancy Drew book again."

—Natasha Small

"Having lost many family members at a young age, I became acquainted with grief early. Bernadine Brown, the protagonist of Beverly Jenkins' Blessings *series, knew where I had been. Bernadine is an intelligent, newly rich Black woman recovering from a painful divorce. Her intelligence, grit, and determination coupled with compassion helped me to weather the storm. She took her riches, bought an ailing town, Henry Adams, in 1800s Kansas, and moved to find a new life. Bernadine was on a mission for rebirth for herself, and for Henry Adams, while I was on a mission of rediscovery. I connected to the deep resolve of many Black women, who believed, 'I can do anything with God and family on my side.'"*

—Albertina Lane

African American women writers have created a canon of literature rooted in the quest to be seen, heard, and healed, a literature now considered a narrative North Star by all who read and depend on stories to give their lives meaning. I came of age as a woman, shaped my voice as a writer, and made my own contributions to that canon as Maya Angelou, Alice Walker, Toni Morrison, Ntozake Shange, Gloria Naylor, and a vast extended family of Black women writers were creating a new vocabulary for the human experience. A language breathtaking in its audacity and originality. Unflinching in its intent and execution.

Many Black women remember exactly who they were in their lives when they first read Maya Angelou's *I Know Why the Caged Bird Sings*. Toni Morrison's *The Bluest Eye* removed the cultural cataracts from the eyes of any reader terrified of bearing witness to the destruction of a small Black girl's soul. Alice Walker educated me about the meaning of courage as she continued to dramatize the violence endured by poor Black Southern women in her short stories and novels, while for many years being scorned and vilified by Black male critics. These women were my contemporaries and my literary sisters. We openly acknowledged the legacy of writers as varied as Phillis Wheatley, Nella Larsen, and Ann Petry, rediscovered their work, introduced it to wider audiences, and praised them for literally making our creative voices possible.

Zora Neale Hurston, novelist, short story writer, anthropologist, playwright, memoirist, and journalist, has become the foremost of our foremothers. Her novel *Their Eyes Were Watching God* heals me anew with each journey into its world. This love story and love letter to Black people contributes to my mental and spiritual well-being.

Set in 1930s Florida, the novel is the story of Janie Crawford's quest to be her own person. This light-skinned, long-haired beauty first marries Logan Killicks, a hard-working farmer who both loves and hates her and her beauty. Her second husband, Joe Starks, a boastful entrepreneur who becomes mayor of an all-Black town, puts her on a pedestal for safe-keeping, choking her will, her voice, and her spirit. After Joe's death, Janie, a thirty-seven-year-old widow, meets and marries Vergible Woods, known as Tea Cake. Tea Cake is a man who introduces her to joy and the undiscovered range of the authority of her own instincts.

This slender novel is panoramic, ambitious, and as satisfying as a Southern Sunday afternoon dinner. There is its recreation of rural Southern culture, manners, speech, and humor, and the ways in which it slyly yet seriously critiques topics like spousal abuse and colorism, weaving that interrogation deftly into the fabric of the story. There is the humanity of the people in the novel. These men and women are cracked, but not broken. The hand of the White man is evident, yet Hurston gives her characters complex lives that in many ways are not and cannot be touched by the White gaze.

Is there any other novel by a Black writer that gives us a love story so affirmative, heartbreaking, and heart-mending? Here is a story that satisfies in so many ways Black women's hunger for love. Our hunger to believe that we can be loved, that we deserve to be loved. For ourselves. Tea Cake's emotional health and vulnerability make him irresistible. He is not perfect. He is a man of his time and his age, and so has touches of chauvinism. Still, Tea Cake's love of Janie is embedded in his belief that she is a woman of boundless, unrealized, and denied potential.

Tea Cake takes Janie into the muck of the Florida Everglades, where they work, live, and love among the common folk. The pair are essentially migrant workers, picking beans and other vegetables among a community of farm laborers who live crop to crop and day to day. Hurston knew these people well for, as an anthropologist, she had lived among them. Dancing in their juke joints, telling tall tales with them, listening to them, studying them, taking them and their culture seriously.

It is among the people on the lowest rung that Janie's confidence grows. Here she is no longer imprisoned in Joe Starks's general store and silenced on the front porch of that store because, as the wife of the mayor, she had to be above everyone else. Here in the "muck," she works hard, loves hard, and becomes part of rather than apart from a community.

As a light-skinned woman, Janie's color thrust her into a caste where she was reviled and envied, where others longed to break her spirit before it bloomed, or to merely say that she was something that they possessed and did not need to know. Holding Tea Cake's hands, Janie meets herself for the first time in her life and likes what she sees. Hurston writes of Janie as she gazes at Tea Cake, "He drifted off into sleep and Janie looked down on him and felt a self-crushing love. So, her soul crawled out from its hiding place."

The Southern dialect is rich, complicated, humorous, and musical. We discover the philosophy, logic, and psychology embedded in the observation about Joe Starks that "Some folks need thrones and ruling chairs and crowns tuh make they influence felt. He don't. He got uh throne in de seat of his pants." The weekend rousing and carousing, the dice games and the knife fights, the drinking, the jesting and joking that characterize life in the camps, are understood as expressions of our human frailty and our glory, and our desperate need for release and relief.

I cherish Janie Crawford because she is symbolic for me of a New Age Strong Black Woman. She learns to trust, to open her heart, and she realizes that she deserves joy, and that happiness is made for her to claim. Emotionally healthy, she leans on her best friend, allows the man who loves her to take care of her, and stands on her own two feet. Vulnerability, uncertainty, and doubt allow her to discover unimagined talents and gifts.

The dominant and oft-repeated metaphor in *Their Eyes Were Watching God* is the horizon, and horizons. Janie Crawford is a woman on the move, travelling with each step toward self-discovery. Traveling guided by a replenishing love. A higher love. A love that convinces me with each reading that, like Janie, I can meet my own shifting horizon and stand in its sunrise.

Coda: New Age Strong Black Women

The stories I have written, discovered, revealed, and shared on this expedition have fortified my faith in and admiration of Black women. We are a mighty force on this earth, in this world. We are more than daunting statistics. No one cares more about our health than we do.

So much of our pride, our identity, and sense of purpose springs from defining ourselves as and being Strong Black Women. Yet the time has come to launch an inquisition into the meaning and cost of a creed that demands unquestioned allegiance. Now we are asking questions. And the questions won't stop. Not until we examine the doctrine of the Strong Black Woman beneath the searchlight of the age we live in, an age that prioritizes well-being over obedience to tradition, self-care over a kneejerk adherence to the image others expect us to project.

I left my doctor's office and launched a search for hard-won answers to unasked questions. I asked Black women who were the Strong Black Women in their lives and what they had learned from them. I asked how much it cost them to be Strong Black Women. I asked how they hurt and how they heal.

As much as this narrative has seemed to be a journey largely through illness and trauma, etched between the lines is the search for the joy that Black women have found and created. Joy is not attained; rather, it is released. It steps forth out of darkness. It withstands assault. We can become New Age Strong Black Women who allow ourselves to lean on others, ask for help, cry when we need to, tend to our souls, and love our families and ourselves. We can become women whose strength is elastic, not made of stone.

Acknowledgements

I want to thank the women who so generously agreed to share a portion of their life stories with me for this book. In our conversations, I would begin with the question, "Who were the Strong Black Women in your life and what did they teach you?" That question launched these women into a backward glance that in some cases revealed contours of their experience and their strength that they had not known or understood until they told their story out loud. I also want to applaud the work of the many healthcare professionals I spoke with, the healers, the activists who helped me grasp the complexity of the Strong Black Woman Complex. I also want to thank Brenda Knight, my editor/publisher, who "got" this book in the format and structure I chose to tell it. Her enthusiasm and commitment made the daunting task of birthing a new story for the world to hear that much easier. And again, thank you to my agent Carol Mann, who has represented me for forty years and believed in this book, as she has in all my books, from the beginning to the end.

About the Author

Marita Golden is a veteran teacher of writing and an acclaimed award-winning author of seventeen works of fiction, nonfiction, and anthologies. As a teacher of writing, she has served as a member of the faculties of the MFA Graduate Creative Writing Programs at George Mason University and Virginia Commonwealth University and in the MA Creative Writing Program at Johns Hopkins University. As a literary consultant, she offers writing workshops, coaching, and manuscript evaluation services.

Books by Marita Golden include the novels *The Wide Circumference of Love*, *After*, and *The Edge of Heaven*, the memoirs *Migrations of the Heart*, *Saving Our Sons*, and *Don't Play in the Sun: One Woman's Journey Through the Color Complex*, and the anthology *Us Against Alzheimer's: Stories of Family Love and Faith*. She is the recipient of many awards, including the Writers for Writers Award presented by Barnes & Noble and Poets and Writers, an award from the Authors Guild, and the Fiction Award for her novel *After* from the Black Caucus of the American Library Association.

As a literary activist, Marita cofounded and serves as President Emerita of the Zora Neale Hurston/Richard Wright Foundation.

Mango Publishing, established in 2014, publishes an eclectic list of books by diverse authors—both new and established voices—on topics ranging from business, personal growth, women's empowerment, LGBTQ studies, health, and spirituality to history, popular culture, time management, decluttering, lifestyle, mental wellness, aging, and sustainable living. We were recently named 2019 *and* 2020's #1 fastest-growing independent publisher by *Publishers Weekly.* Our success is driven by our main goal, which is to publish high-quality books that will entertain readers as well as make a positive difference in their lives.

Our readers are our most important resource; we value your input, suggestions, and ideas. We'd love to hear from you—after all, we are publishing books for you!

Please stay in touch with us and follow us at:
Facebook: Mango Publishing
Twitter: @MangoPublishing
Instagram: @MangoPublishing
LinkedIn: Mango Publishing
Pinterest: Mango Publishing
Newsletter: mangopublishinggroup.com/newsletter

Join us on Mango's journey to reinvent publishing, one book at a time.

9 781642 506839